How Your Horse
MOVES

A unique visual guide to improving performance

Gillian Higgins with Stephanie Martin

DAVID & CHARLES

www.davidandcharles.com

This book is dedicated to Freddie and Quake.

Two very special horses to whom I owe my

passion for anatomy and biomechanics.

A DAVID AND CHARLES BOOK
© David and Charles, Ltd 2009

David and Charles is an imprint of David and Charles, Ltd,
Suite A, Tourism House, Pynes Hill, Exeter, EX2 5WS

First published in the UK and USA in 2009

Text and illustrations copyright © Gillian Higgins 2009

Photographs on pages 4, 5, 7, 8, 9, 10, 11, 14 (top), 18, 19
(pull out image 4), 25 (lower right), 27 (lower), 28 (lower
right), 34 (top right), 35 (lower left), 38, 39 (top left and
lower left), 43 (top and lower right), 44 (lower left), 46
(left), 51 (right), 52 (right), 54 (lower right), 55 (top right),
58 (lower), 62 (lower), 65 (right), 66 (top), 67, 68, 72, 73, 74
(top), 75 (top left and top right), 79 (top right), 80, 81, 85
(right), 86, 87 (top), 88 (lower left, top right and lower right),
100 (left and lower right), 101 (right), 102 (left), 103 (lower
left and lower right), 105 (top) 112 (left), 113, 114, 115, 116,
117, 121, 122, 123 (top), 124, 126, 128, 130, 131, 132, 134,
135, 136, 137 (right), 138, 139, 140, 141, 142, 143, 147 (top
right and lower right), 148 (right), 149 (lower left and right),
151 and 152 © Gillian Higgins 2009.

Photographs on pages 13, 15, 16, 17, 20, 25 (top left), 27
(top), 28 (lower left), 37 (right), 44 (right), 45 (left), 46
(right), 47 (lower), 48 (lower), 49 (lower left and top right),
50, 51 (left), 52 (left), 54 (left and top right), 55 (lower
right), 57, 58 (right), 59 (middle and lower), 63 (lower), 64
(lower left and lower right), 65 (left), 66 (lower), 70 (top
right and lower right), 71, 76 (right and lower left), 83, 84
(lower right), 85 (bottom left), 87 (lower), 88 (top left), 89
(left), 96, 97, 101 (lower left), 105 (middle), 111, 120, 137
(left), 146 (left), 147, 148 (top left, middle left and lower
left), 149 (top left) and 150 © Horsepix 2009. With its roots
in horse country and staffed by horse people, Horsepix is a
leading provider of high quality equestrian photography.

Photographs on pages 6, 14, (lower), 19 (main and pullout
images 1–3 and 5), 22, 23, 24, 25 (lower left and top right),
26, 27 (middle) 28 (top left and right), 29, 30, 31, 32, 33, 34
(left and lower right), 35 (top left and right), 36, 37 (left),
39 (right), 40, 42, 43 (lower left), 44 (top left), 45 (top right
and lower right), 47 (top), 48 (top), 49 (top left and lower
left) 53 (lower), 55 (left), 56, 57 (left and lower right), 59
(top), 60, 61, 62 (top), 63 (top), 64 (top right), 69, 70 (left),
74 (lower), 75 (lower), 76 (lower), 78 (right), 82, 84 (left and
top right), 85 (top and middle left), 86 (right), 90, 91,

92, 93, 94, 95, 98, 99, 100 (top right), 101 (top left), 102
(top right and lower right), 103 (top left and top right),
104, 105 (bottom), 106, 107, 108, 109, 110, 112 (right),
123 (lower), 127, 129 and 133 (left) taken by Horsepix,
© David and Charles, Ltd 2009.

Gillian Higgins has asserted her right to be identified as
author of this work in accordance with the Copyright,
Designs and Patents Act, 1988.

A catalogue record for this book is available from the
British Library.

ISBN-13: 978-1-4463-0099-2 paperback

Commissioning Editor: Jane Trollope
Desk Editor: Emily Rae
Copy Editor: Kim Bryan
Senior Designer: Jodie Lystor
Production Controller: Beverley Richardson

David and Charles publishes high-quality books on a
wide range of subjects. For more information visit
www.davidandcharles.com.

CONTENTS

FOREWORD

I first met Gillian as a fellow competitor on the eventing circuit and after my Olympic horse Ringwood Cockatoo experienced some muscle problems. I approached Gillian to come and treat him, knowing that she has a very high reputation in treating horses and also great knowledge about the different jobs an event horse has to excel at.

I have been competing at International Level since 1982 and also train many other top event riders from numerous different countries. I have represented my country, Germany, at nine European Championships, four World Equestrian Games and three Olympic Games.

When Gillian came to treat Ringwood Cockatoo, I made sure that I was present to watch her working and also to talk about her philosophy. Being a top athlete myself, I am aware of the importance of certain muscle groups that are used whilst in the saddle, in particular to core stability, which is vital to be able to maintain good balance.

Interestingly Gillian and I shared the same strong views on the way muscles are used in both the rider and in the horse. With riding you always have ups and downs and these are often down to your horse being injured.

By reading *How your Horse Moves* and putting into practice Gillian's thoughts, ideas and concepts I strongly believe that you can reduce unnecessary damage to your horse, be this by getting them fitter, or stronger, or just more balanced.

Obviously only a perfectly balanced rider will be able to train a horse to reach the top level of its chosen discipline and only a perfectly balanced horse will be capable of doing so.

Gillian is gifted in her ability to see and explain what others cannot within a horse. Her lecture demonstrations are thoroughly entrancing and you cannot help but come away with something new to try out. The 300 photographs and illustrations in *How Your Horse Moves* show the anatomy of the horse and its biomechanics, making it very visual and easy to understand.

It doesn't matter what level or discipline you ride in or even if you are preparing for an exam, this book should be read by anyone interested in having a full understanding of the horse.

BETTINA HOY

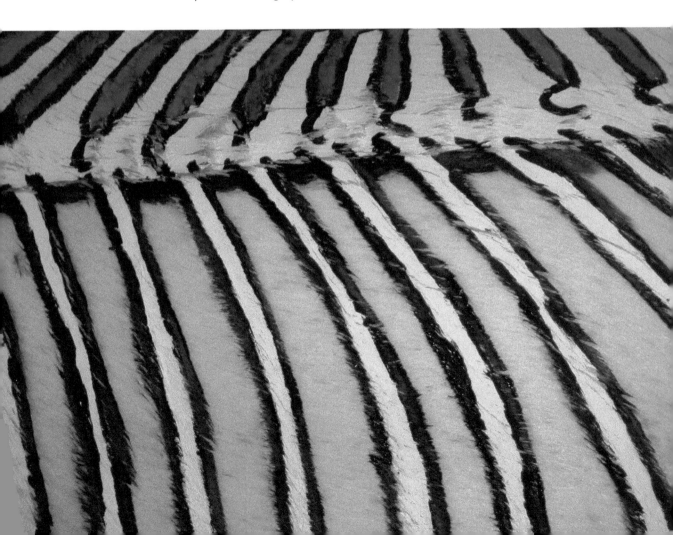

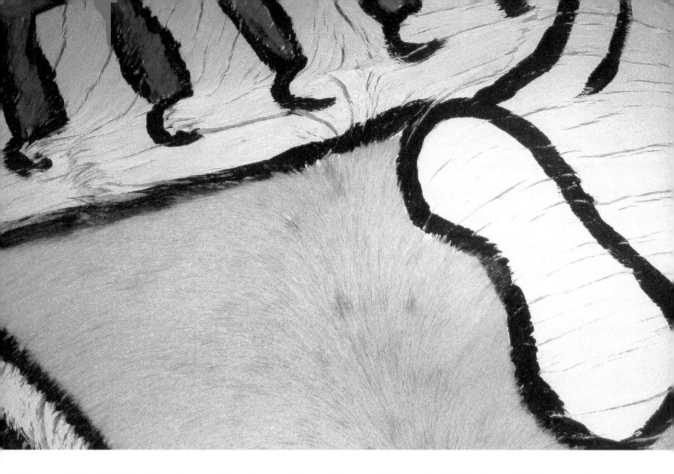

I first met Gillian Higgins when she came for training with her event horses as a young rider in about 2000. She showed a talent and interest then, not just in competing her horses but also in understanding the system of training. As a trainer I have always wanted to first understand the logic behind a system of training and then to explain to riders, not just what to do but why it makes sense to do it. An understanding of the biomechanics helps a rider to train more sympathetically as well as more effectively. Gillian's obvious interest in the 'why' as well as the 'what' led to her going on to train as an Equine Remedial Therapist.

Having seen Gillian's 'Horses Inside Out' presentation, when I was asked if I would read her book, I was immediately interested and not disappointed. The step-by-step, thorough explanation of the musculoskeletal system and its relationship to schooling and conditioning the sport horse is both sufficiently detailed for the serious student whilst being easy to read and follow. The book is attractively laid out with clever use of live 'models' to show how the various components of the horse's body function and develop during a horse's sporting career. I especially like the 'Top Tips' and the summaries at the end of each section.

Gillian's knowledge of the principles of training combined with the understanding of how the musculoskeletal system functions enables her to offer useful advice and tips on schooling. The sections on 'The Way of Going' and 'The Gaits' help to clarify the relationship between the expressions used in training and dressage judging to the form and function of the horse's body.

As any of us who have participated in sport know, we will be affected by muscle soreness as a result of exercise and we all benefit from deep massage and stretching exercises. The horse is no different so the sections describing common problems and then on how to persuade the horse to perform useful stretching exercises by using a combination of carrot and reflexes is very practical. If performed regularly, it is also useful in assessing if there are any musculoskeletal problems or changes that are the root cause of schooling difficulties. Professional help can then be called upon before the problem causes a mental block on the part of the horse.

The brief section on choice of horse is not just helpful in finding and purchasing a horse but also in understanding where the horse may struggle to perform when their conformation or type does not lend itself ideally to a chosen discipline. The combination of this understanding together with correct and sympathetic training will enable riders and trainers to get the most out of the horse that they have.

I am always looking for books and other ideas to recommend to my students to improve their understanding of how a horse performs and the logic of the training system. This will certainly be one of them.

CHRISTOPHER BARTLE

'Why is an anatomy lesson worth your time – time you perhaps feel is better spent actually riding your horse? It is my feeling that in order to truly consider oneself a rider one must be educated in the horse's basic physiology, conformation and behaviour. If you know how the horse is built, how its skeletal, muscular and ligament systems work together, and how its actions are controlled in part by instinct along with other aspects of the mind, then it only follows that you know better how to ride it.'

Dr Gerd Heuschmann
Tug of War
Classical versus 'Modern' Dressage, 2006, translated 2007

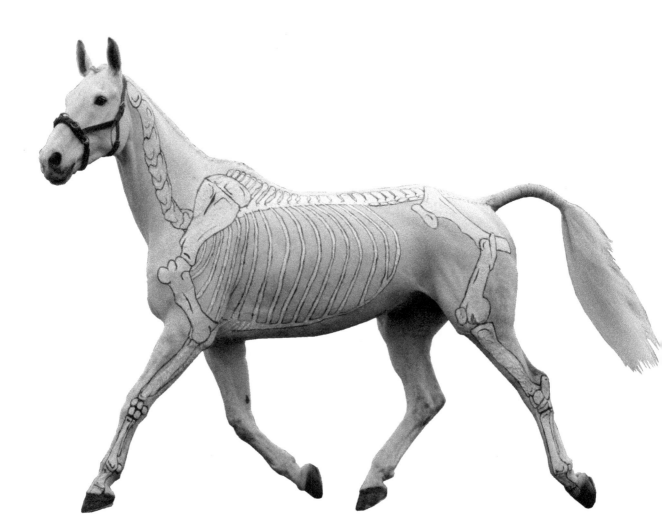

INTRODUCTION

This book is all about getting the best from your horse, improving his performance and more importantly his welfare. Not every horse is going to be a world beater and many disappointments could be averted if riders' understood how and why their horses move in the way they do. It would enable them to accept physical limitations, train with empathy, achieve realistic goals and bring out the best in their horse.

As a therapist, I constantly see horses with muscle imbalances and tension, caused by rider imbalance, asymmetrical muscle development or by expecting too much too soon from a horse whose musculature is not up to the challenge. For a horse to perform well, it takes time for the musculoskeletal system to develop the appropriate strength for the task, time to learn to balance both himself and the rider and time to assimilate that which he is being asked. The rider needs the time and patience to forge a

relationship with his horse. This requires empathy, tact and respect. Time spent in this way is never lost. It is far better to prevent a problem than to have to find a cure.

Seeing the musculature and skeleton painted on the horse enables riders to see how the horse moves from an anatomical perspective. The unique artwork used in Horses Inside Out lecture demonstrations provides a living equine canvas that shows how bones and muscles work together to produce movement. The reaction to these lectures has been overwhelming and comments such as 'I wish I had known this 20 years ago!' I have ridden all my life and now everything I have been taught has fallen into place!' are not uncommon.

The book is divided into three sections:
- **Part one** looks at the component parts of the musculoskeletal system and takes the reader on an anatomical journey through the technical aspects of 'How Your Horse Moves'. It is designed to inform readers of the basic principles that will be referred to in the text that follows
- **Part two** looks at various applied aspects of 'How Your Horse Moves', from how he bends and jumps to how he uses his limbs and maintains an outline. This basic understanding can be very useful in riding, training, analysing ways of going, improving performance and caring for your horse
- **Part three** suggests ways in which the reader can keep the horse moving freely, paying particular attention to the musculoskeletal system. It contains a wealth of practical advice and suggestions showing the reader how the horse's musculature can be maintained in optimum condition.

The book is designed either to be read as a whole, or to be dipped into as required. Although there are suggestions on how to achieve some of the desirable qualities required for good movement, it is not intended to be a training manual. It attempts to explain how and why the horse moves as he does. We all want our horses to perform to the best of their abilities but ultimately it is up to us to be sensitive to their individual requirements, physical capabilities and wellbeing.

ACKNOWLEDGMENTS
I would like to thank my father David for his photography, IT support and for providing an oasis of calm at times of stress. I would especially like to thank Caroline Moore who has taught me so much, has been and continues to be an inspiration. Finally, thanks go to my friend Sam Rahmatalla and her beautiful Grand Prix dressage horse Bungle and to my horses for their patience.

A FIRM FOUNDATION

Before we can really understand how our horses move, we need a sound knowledge of the component parts that make up the musculoskeletal system.

This chapter covers:

• bones

• muscle make up

• fascinating fascia

• tendons and ligaments

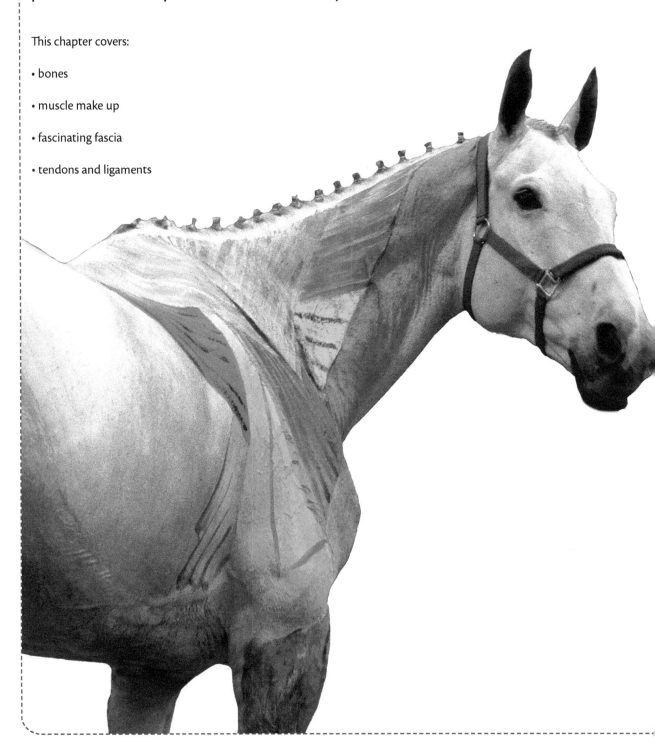

BONES

Bone is living tissue with nerves and blood vessels that contains proteins and minerals, such as calcium and phosphorus. The horse must receive adequate amounts of these minerals to remain healthy. Bone is the second hardest substance in the horse's body after tooth enamel.

A bone consists of a hard outer cortex, encasing a spongy cavity. The surface of the bone is covered by the periosteum, a tough protective membrane, which provides for the attachment of ligaments and tendons. (See illustration of cross-section of a synovial joint on page 11.)

The skeleton is made up of a combination of bones classified as:	
Long bones	These are literally long bones that contain marrow. They manufacture new blood cells, and have joint surfaces at either end. Operated by muscles and joints, they act as levers for the appendicular skeleton. Examples are the cannon, femur, radius and ulna, and humerus.
Short bones	Short bones are strong and compact. Some examples are the short pasterns, the carpal bones in the knee, and the tarsal bones in the hock.
Flat bones	Flat bones have broad, flat surfaces that enclose and protect organs and provide a large area for muscle attachment. The ribs, skull, scapula, and sternum are examples of flat bones.
Sesamoid bones	Sesamoid bones lie within tendons or ligaments and add strength to them. An example is the navicular bone working within the deep digital flexor tendon. The sesamoid bones lie behind the bones of the fetlock and help to keep the tendons and ligaments in that area functioning correctly.
Irregular bones	The vertebral column consists of irregular bones. These protect the central nervous system.

The skeleton

The skeletal system of the horse consists of approximately 205 bones divided into:

- the axial skeleton comprising the skull, vertebrae, sternum and ribs
- the appendicular skeleton which is made up of the fore and hind limb bones.

The number of bones varies as some fuse together as the horse matures and because the number of tail bones varies from horse to horse.

Functions of the skeleton

The skeleton has five major functions. These are:

- **to act as support**. The skeleton provides a stable and rigid framework for the attachment of muscles and tendons
- **to assist movement**. When skeletal muscles contract, they pull on bones to produce movement
- **to protect the internal organs**
- **to produce and store blood cells** in the bone marrow
- **to store minerals**, especially calcium and phosphorus, which contribute to bone strength.

The skull protects the brain.

What is a joint?

A joint allows movement. It is the area where two or more bones meet. They are stabilized by a complex network of tendons, ligaments, and muscles. Movement is dependant on the contraction and relaxation of muscles and the associated articulation of the joints.

Understanding the relationship between the skeleton and muscles helps us understand how our horses move.

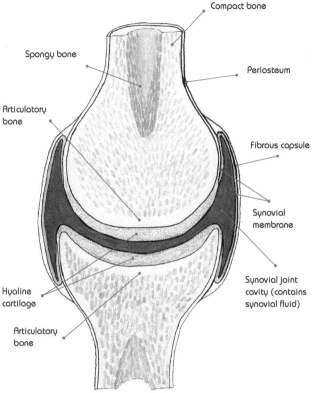

Compact bone

Spongy bone

Articulatory bone

Periosteum

Fibrous capsule

Synovial membrane

Hyaline cartilage

Synovial joint cavity (contains synovial fluid)

Articulatory bone

Cross-section of a synovial joint.

Cartilage is a dense connective tissue containing collagen and elastic fibres covering the ends of bones at some joints. It reduces friction within the joint and aids shock absorption. It contains no blood vessels or nerves.

Joints can be classified as:
- **fibrous**, where bones are held by fibrous connective tissue. There is no joint cavity and little movement, an example is the skull
- **cartilaginous**, which are held together by cartilage. These joints have little articulation or movement. Important examples are the pelvis and the larger joint surfaces between vertebral bodies
- **synovial**, which are fully moveable, modified shock absorbers. They are composed of a fibrous capsule, ligaments, and a joint lining, which manufactures lubricating synovial fluid. The ends of the bones are lined with hyaline cartilage, which provides a smooth surface between the bones and compresses to act as a shock absorber; for example, when taking off or landing after a jump. This type of joint is the most active, therefore most susceptible to injury. The fetlock is a synovial joint.

There are two main types of synovial joint:
- **ball and socket** – the ball-shaped end of the bone sits in its socket and is able to move in almost any direction. Examples are the shoulder and hip joints.

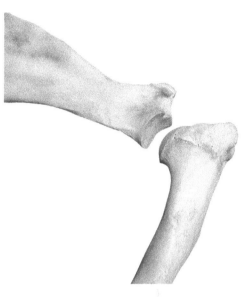

- **hinge** – these resemble an opening door. They allow flexion and extension in one plane only. The elbow and pastern joints are examples of hinge joints.

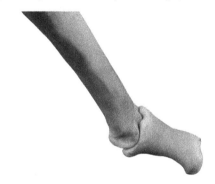

SUMMARY
- **Bones are the hard living tissue that forms the skeleton.**
- **They can be classified by shape.**
- **The skeleton provides support, produces movement, protects internal organs, and manufactures blood cells.**
- **Joints are the point at which bones meet.**
- **They allow movement.**
- **Joints are stabilized by muscles, tendons and ligaments.**

MUSCLE MAKE UP

There are three types of muscle found within the body:
- **cardiac**, which is specific to the heart and cannot be consciously controlled
- **smooth**, which is also involuntary and plays a part in the circulatory and digestive systems
- **skeletal**, which produces movement, maintains posture, and stabilizes joints. This muscle type is under conscious control although it will contract involuntarily as a reflex response.

More about skeletal muscle

Skeletal muscles come in all shapes and sizes. They respond to motor nerve impulses, are highly elastic, and have strong contractile power.

Muscles have a fleshy 'belly' comprising thousands of muscle fibres intertwined with connective tissue called fascia (page 14). Muscle fibres decrease towards the ends of a muscle, reducing its circumference until only the longitudinally arranged collagen fibres remain in the form of a tendon. This attaches to the bone via a tough fibrous membrane known as the periosteum. Muscles are attached to, and therefore move the skeleton by passing over joints (see page 16).

The points at which the skeletal muscles attach to the bones via the tendons are known as:
- the point of **origin** – nearest to the body centre
- the point of **insertion** – furthest away from the body centre.

Skeletal muscles – up close

Muscles consist of fibres made up of many thousands of individual muscle cells that run parallel to each other. The fibres are bound together in bundles, called fascicles, by very thin layers of connective fascia.

Within each fibre are thousands of smaller threads known as myofibrils, which give the muscle its ability to lengthen and shorten. Within the myofibrils are millions of minute bands known as sarcomeres, which comprise myofilaments made up of proteins. Actin produces thin myofilaments and myosin produces thick ones. These are responsible for muscle contraction. They slide over one another when the muscles contract thereby shortening it. They slide back to their original position as the muscle relaxes.

THERE ARE APPROXIMATELY 700 SKELETAL MUSCLES IN THE HORSE!

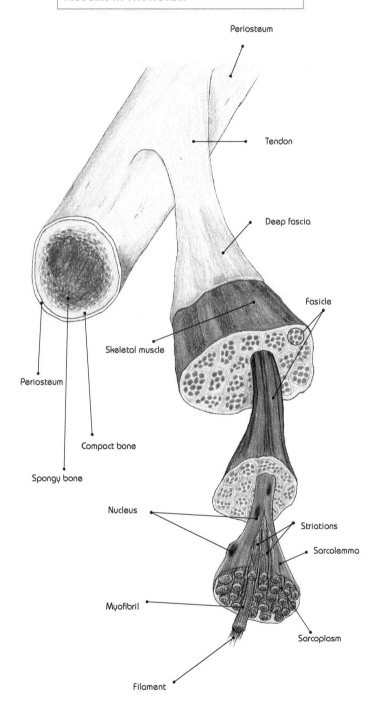

Periosteum

Tendon

Deep fascia

Fasicle

Skeletal muscle

Periosteum

Compact bone

Spongy bone

Nucleus

Striations

Sarcolemma

Myofibril

Sarcoplasm

Filament

Very simply, muscles convert chemical energy into movement. Skeletal muscle fibres come in different types. These are inherited, so although you can train to get the best from your horse, you can not actually change them. In other words you cannot change a cob into a racehorse any more than you can change a weight lifter into a long distance runner!

The muscle types are:
- **slow twitch** that produce energy slowly over a long period. They work aerobically, requiring oxygen to create energy. Horses with a predominance of these types of muscle fibres are less likely to fatigue and are good for endurance
- **fast twitch** that are physically larger than slow twitch fibres. They work anaerobically producing small amounts of energy quickly and explosively but they tire out easily. Horses with muscles that have a predominance of fast twitch fibres are good for jumping.

Like people, all horses have a combination of both types of muscle fibre. It is a predominance of one fibre type that determines activity.

In show jumpers fast twitch fibres predominate.

Endurance horses have a predominance of slow twitch fibres.

SUMMARY
- Skeletal muscle produces movement, stabilizes joints, and maintains posture.
- Muscles have a fleshy belly that tapers into a tendon at the distal end.
- They have a point of origin and a point of insertion where they attach to bone.
- Muscle has slow twitch fibres, which contract slowly but keep going for a long time, and fast twitch fibres, which contract quickly but tire rapidly.

FASCINATING FASCIA

The uninterrupted web of soft tissue that permeates and surrounds every muscle, bone and organ in the body, binding it together and allowing it to operate as one homogenous unit, is called the fascia. It is the high density of collagen fibres within the fascia that gives it strength, elastic properties and resilience.

The **superficial fascia**, separates muscle from the skin and underlying structures and provides a pathway for lymph, nerves and blood vessels to enter the muscles. It also serves as an insulating layer, reducing heat loss and cushioning the muscles from physical trauma.

The **deep fascia** is dense, irregular connective tissue that penetrates, surrounds, and holds together the muscles, ligaments, tendons, joint capsules, periosteum, bones, nerves and blood vessels. Each bundle of muscle is wrapped in a thin, tight sheath of fascia until it reaches its required bulk. The muscle fibres then reduce, narrowing in circumference and continuing as tendons.

Fascia consists of several layers of overlapping, interwoven tissue named after their location, for example gluteal, thoracolumbar, or omobrachial.

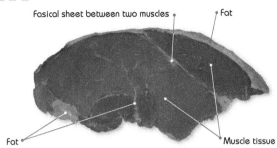

Fascial sheet between two muscles · · Fat

Fat · · Muscle tissue

In appearance the fascia is opaque, clingy and slightly stretchy. When you pull a raw chicken apart the fascia is the strong sheet of white glistening material that you see.

The role of the fascia

Fascia strengthens, provides support and protection, and acts as a shock absorber for the muscles. In its optimal condition, it is loose, moist and mobile; it provides an area for muscle attachment, assists the movement of muscles, and allows individual muscles to slide against each other without interference.

Gluteal fascia

Thoracolumbar fascia

Dorsoscapular ligament within the thoracolumbar fascia

Fascia Lata

Cervical fascia

Femoral fascia

Omobrachial fascia

Antebrachial fascia

Crural fascia

Abdominal fascia

Faulty fascia!

When damaged or strained, the fascia becomes less flexible and more inelastic, rather like wearing tight restrictive clothing, which limits your range of movement.

Because of its interconnecting nature, when one part is damaged, it can affect structures far removed from the original site of the injury.

Training requires a combination of flexibility, strength, balance, endurance, and coordination. Any or all of these components may be adversely affected when fascial restrictions occur.

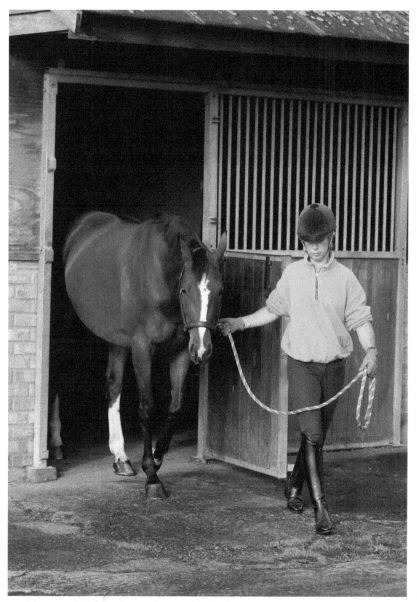

Problems with the fascia are often overlooked when a horse seems stiff or sore.

SUMMARY

- Fascia is a continuous sheath of connective tissue that provides structural support for the skeleton and soft tissues.
- The membrane connects all structures of the body.
- The tendons and ligaments are made up of the same collagen fibres as the fascia.

TENDONS AND LIGAMENTS

Tendons are formed when the muscle bulk reduces. They are dense, fibrous, parallel bundles of collagen arranged in long cords that have high tensile strength but limited elasticity. The structure of tendons is slightly zig zag or crimped. Tendons are energy saving in nature as they have the ability to stretch and recoil.

A ligament is a band of connective tissue which holds either bones or some tendons in place. They have less stretch than tendons. Ligaments stabilize and protect every joint in the body, including those of the vertebral column, pelvis, hip, stifle and lower limbs.

Tendons

Tendons attach skeletal muscle to bone and, as part of the muscle/tendon unit, they facilitate movement.

Tendons have certain properties:
- they are relatively inelastic in comparison to muscles but are more elastic than ligaments. Their high tensile strength enables them to withstand enormous loads
- they insert into the periosteum of the bone by means of small spikes known as 'Sharpey's fibres'
- they have a point of origin, which is the parent muscle, and a point of insertion where they attach into bone
- they can be short, for example the tendons in the trunk of the body, or long, such as the tendons in the lower leg
- they are protected by tendon sheaths or fluid-filled sacs called bursae.

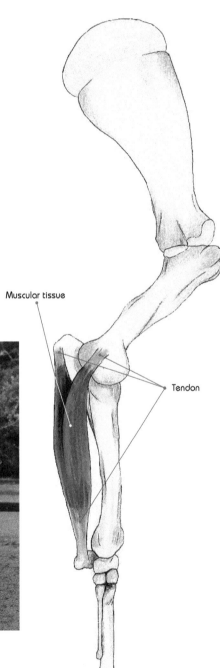

Muscular tissue

Tendon

Tendons that are well defined are also healthy.

Ligaments

Ligaments connect bone to bone. They differ from a tendon in not being part of a muscle.

Their properties include:
• supporting the joint and preventing it from over-extending, over-flexing, or over-rotating
• being made of collagen, a protein found in connective tissue. They are stronger than tendons
• a limited blood supply, which makes them slow to heal when damaged.

There are four different types of ligament.
1. Those that support or suspend, for example the suspensory ligament.
2. Annular, which wrap around the joint. These consist of broad bands of ligament that direct the pull on a tendon. An example is the annular ligament of the fetlock joint
3. Inter-osseus, which link bones together, for example the interspinous ligaments in between the spinous processes of the vertebrae.
4. Funicular, which help hold the bones together, for example the funicular part of the nuchal ligament.

As there are no muscles below the knee, both tendons and ligaments here are long and susceptible to damage.

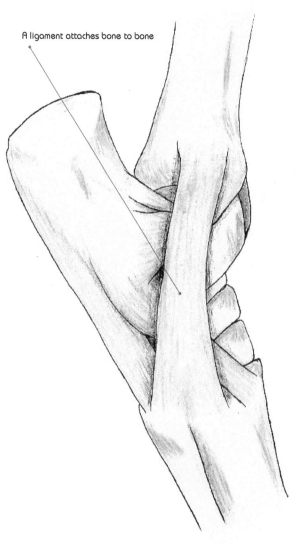

A ligament attaches bone to bone

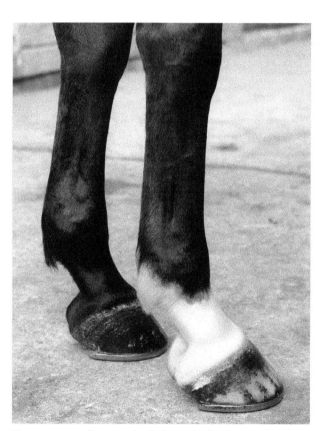

The suspensory ligament in the lower leg is often confused with bone.

SUMMARY
• **Tendons attach muscle to bone and are involved in movement.**
• **Ligaments join bone to bone and control the joint.**

THE NEXT LEVEL

Each of the component parts that make up the horse's musculoskeletal system link together, forming a strong, flexible structure.

This chapter covers:

• the horse's spine

• the head and neck

• the back

• the lumbo-sacral junction, pelvis and the sacroiliac joint

• from hip to hock

• from scapula to knee

• below the knee

• no foot, no horse!

THE HORSE'S SPINE

The horse's backbone is part of the axial skeleton. It is made up of vertebrae that run down the horse's midline dorsally, providing stability and protecting the spinal cord.

The axial skeleton

The horse's skeleton, excluding the limbs, is known as the axial skeleton. It comprises eight parts.

1. Skull
2. Seven cervical vertebrae
3. Eighteen thoracic vertebrae
4. Six lumbar vertebrae
5. Five fused sacral vertebrae
6. Between eighteen and twenty-two caudal vertebrae
7. Ribs
8. Sternum

General features of the spine

- There are between 54 and 58 vertebrae, lying one behind the other from the base of skull to the end of the dock. Their primary function is to encase and protect the spinal cord. They also provide points of attachment for the muscles, tendons and ligaments that support the weight of the body.
- Vertebrae are classified as irregular bones because they are all slightly different and fit together rather like a jigsaw puzzle. Moving along the spine from the head towards the tail, each vertebra changes slightly so it is different from its neighbour.
- The spine, apart from the neck and tail is an inflexible structure capable of only minor adjustments either up and down or laterally, from side to side. This rigidity supports the weighty trunk, which contains the large intestine found in all grazing animals. The spine cannot curl, which means the horse is unable to roll itself in to a ball like a cat!

The horse's spine.

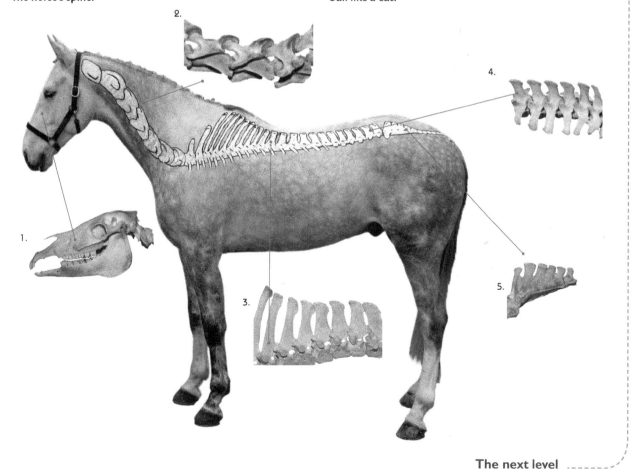

- Between each vertebra there are small fibro-cartilaginous pads, which when compressed, allow slight movement. The vertebrae are held together by strong ligaments and small deep muscular attachments, which criss-cross between themselves and each other, stabilizing the spine and maintaining posture. The strength of the spine is derived from a combination of the vertebrae, cartilage, muscles and ligaments.

- The bones of the spine from the poll to tail are linked by, the **multifidus muscle**. This is a composite muscle made up of a number of separate units each spanning between two and six vertebrae. It is the main deep muscle responsible for aligning and stabilizing individual joints and making small postural adjustments along the entire length of the spine from the second cervical vertebra (the axis) through to the end of the tail. Short fibres attach from the side of each vertebra and insert via several branches into the top of the neighbouring vertebrae.

- The longissimus dorsi muscle is the longest muscle in the horse's body. It runs the full length of the back from the last few cervical vertebrae to the pelvis and sacrum. It helps define the topline and is the muscle on which we sit. It is responsible for extending the spine (dipping the back) and raising and supporting the head and neck. It is the main muscle used in turning, rearing, kicking and jumping.

There is a minimal amount of sideways bend through the length of the spine but, when a horse turns its head to its flank, most of the bend comes from the neck.

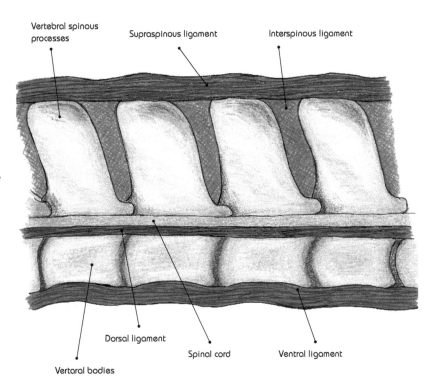

Vertebral spinous processes   Supraspinous ligament   Interspinous ligament

Dorsal ligament   Spinal cord   Ventral ligament

Vertaral bodies

Cross-section showing the ligament support of the spine.

The multifidus muscle.

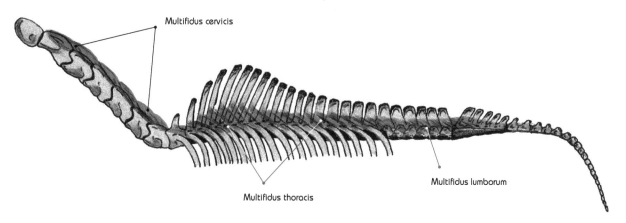

Multifidus cervicis

Multifidus thoracis

Multifidus lumborum

The longissimus dorsi muscle.

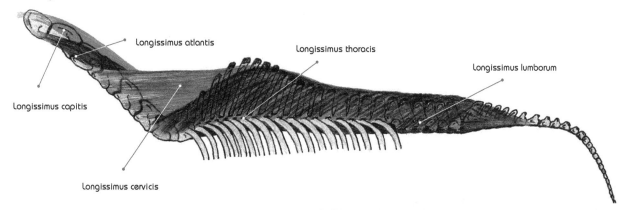

Longissimus atlantis

Longissimus thoracis

Longissimus lumborum

Longissimus capitis

Longissimus cervicis

The common structural plan

Although adjacent vertebrae may differ in size, shape and detail, they all share the same basic features.

Vertebral canal. This is the area through which the spinal cord runs. It is created by the vertebral body below and the vertebral arch above. Notches in the vertebral arch align with those in the adjacent vertebrae, creating an aperture exactly the right size for a spinal nerve to exit

Spinous process. This is a single bony projection, which extends dorsally or upwards from a vertebra providing an area for muscle attachment

Articular processes. Each vertebra has four articular processes. These are small projections linking adjacent vertebrae to make the spine more stable. They are coated with cartilage creating smooth synovial, facet joints

Vertebral body. This is the thick, disk-shaped lower portion that is 'weight bearing'. In humans, the vertebral bodies are stacked vertically. In the horse, they are horizontal and the forces are more like those of a suspension bridge

Transverse processes. These are the bony projections that extend laterally, or sideways from a vertebra to provide an area of muscle attachment

The next level

THE HEAD AND NECK

The head and neck together account for about 10 per cent of the horse's body weight. The head needs to be large to accommodate the jaws and teeth necessary for grazing. The neck needs to be long to enable the horse to graze and to allow self-grooming. The head and neck acts like a giant pendulum, which has huge implications for movement, balance and distribution of weight. By adjusting the position of the head and neck, the horse can alter its centre of gravity. The neck is the most flexible part of the horse's spine.

The head

The function of the skull is to protect the brain, eyes, inner parts of the ear and nasal passages. It is made up of flat bones joined together by fibrous joints. These joints ossify as the horse becomes older.

The mobile mandible, or lower jaw, joins to the skull at the temporomandibular joint and is used for chewing. When a ridden horse fixes or 'crosses' his jaw, it causes tension through his jaw muscles stiffening the temporomandibular joint. This in turn can lead to tension in the neck muscles.

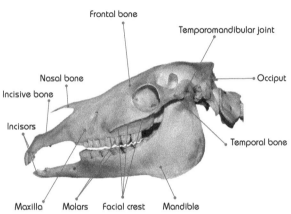

The neck

The head joins on to the neck at the poll. The first and second neck vertebrae are the atlas and axis, which are anatomically very different both from each other and the other five neck vertebrae. The vertebral canal, the large channel running through them, allows for the safe passage of the spinal cord in an area with a considerable range of movement.

The vertebrae of the cervical region have much reduced spinous and transverse processes. The top surfaces are rough where they allow for the attachment of strong muscles and the nuchal ligament, which support the weight of the head and neck.

The cervical vertebrae are situated considerably lower than many people imagine. They do not follow the topline.

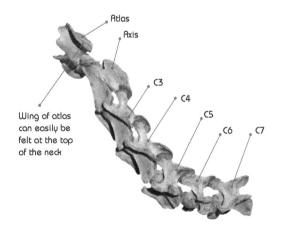

Articulation of the head and neck

Articulation refers to movement at a joint. As the most flexible part of the spine, the cervical vertebrae have considerable scope for movement, most of which occurs at the base of the neck when the head is raised or lowered. Movement of the vertebrae along its length allows for lateral curvature and arching.

The first cervical vertebra, called the atlas, articulates with the skull at the occiput and allows the horse to 'nod' its head. The wing of the atlas can be felt on either side of the neck below the poll.

The second cervical vertebra, called the axis, which is attached to the atlas by a tooth like projection allows the horse to twist his head from side to side. Both movements are explained in more detail on pages 69–70.

The nuchal ligament

The nuchal ligament is one of the most important structures in the horse's body. It is a strong, elastic, rope-like ligament, made from fibrous material with a relatively poor blood supply, which runs from the poll to the top of the spinous processes at the withers.

The nuchal ligament has several major functions including:
- helping to support the weight of the head and neck, holding it in position
- acting as an energy saving device by reducing the amount of muscular effort needed to support the weight of the head
- allowing the head and neck to be raised and lowered
- restraining and stabilizing the movement of the spinous processes at the highest point of the withers
- maintaining the correct alignment of the cervical vertebrae.

The nuchal ligament has two parts:
1. the **funicular** part consists of two parallel cords that run along the nuchal crest from the occipital bone to the top of the spinous processes at the withers
2. the **lamellar** part is made up of finger-like projections that run from the funicular cord to the tops of the cervical neck vertebrae below it.

The nuchal ligament continues as the supraspinous ligament, linking the tops of each vertebral spinous process from the withers to the end of the sacrum.

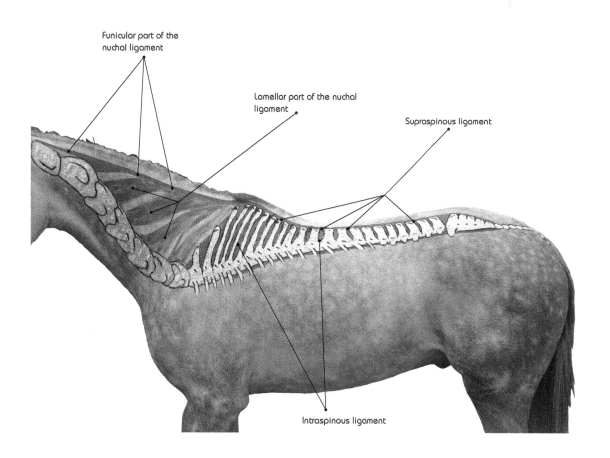

Funicular part of the nuchal ligament

Lamellar part of the nuchal ligament

Supraspinous ligament

Intraspinous ligament

Main muscle movers of the neck

The muscles of the neck work across several joints simultaneously. They can be divided into two types:
• superficial muscles, mainly the extensors and flexors, which are responsible for large gymnastic movements. These tend to be big, bulky and provide power

• deep seated muscles, including the multifidus cervicis, which are mainly responsible for the postural control of the joints.

Three of the main superficial muscles in the neck.

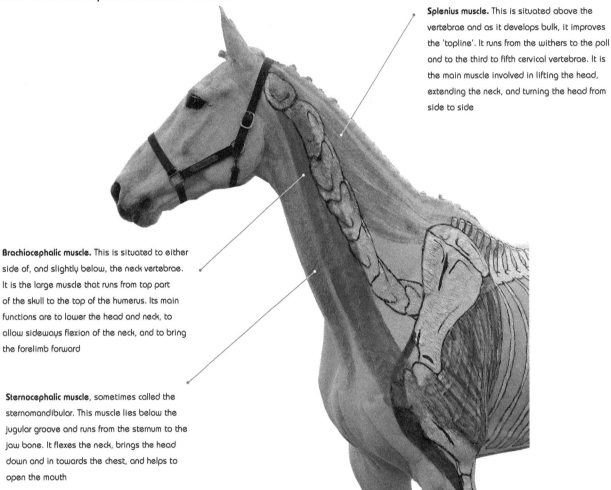

Splenius muscle. This is situated above the vertebrae and as it develops bulk, it improves the 'topline'. It runs from the withers to the poll and to the third to fifth cervical vertebrae. It is the main muscle involved in lifting the head, extending the neck, and turning the head from side to side

Brachiocephalic muscle. This is situated to either side of, and slightly below, the neck vertebrae. It is the large muscle that runs from top part of the skull to the top of the humerus. Its main functions are to lower the head and neck, to allow sideways flexion of the neck, and to bring the forelimb forward

Sternocephalic muscle, sometimes called the sternomandibular. This muscle lies below the jugular groove and runs from the sternum to the jaw bone. It flexes the neck, brings the head down and in towards the chest, and helps to open the mouth

SUMMARY
• **The head and neck account for 10 per cent of the horse's body weight.**
• **The neck is the most flexible part of the horse's spine.**
• **The neck vertebrae are lower than most people realize.**
• **The nuchal ligament supports the head and neck. It is one of the most important structures in the horse's body.**

THE BACK

The horse's spine is a strong and complex structure, consisting of the thoracic and lumbar vertebrae, which are supported by a myriad of ligaments and muscles.

The thoracic spine

This consists of 18 vertebrae each separated by a fibrous intervertebral disc and locked together by articular processes. With only one or two degrees of movement between each joint, it is a very rigid area.

The rigid nature of the horse's spine is what allows us to sit on and ride our horses.

The spinal column runs lower than many people imagine. This is due to the fact that each vertebral body is topped by a spinous process of up to 25cm (10in), the longest being on the fourth and fifth thoracic vertebrae which create the withers. These processes then decrease in length towards the tail. They provide extensive areas for muscle and ligament attachment as well as acting as levers for movement particularly at the withers. The tops of the spinous processes can be felt as knobbly 'bumps' along the midline of the horse's back.

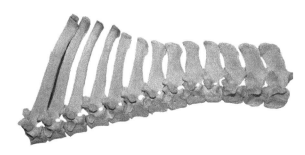

The area of the back on which we sit.

Eighteen pairs of ribs insert between neighbouring thoracic vertebrae via synovial joints before protruding horizontally to curve round the barrel of the horse. The first eight pairs, which house and protect the heart and lungs, are known as true ribs. They join on to the sternum ventrally and allow the chest cavity to expand and deflate as the horse breathes. The other ten pairs are known as false ribs as each pair attaches by a ligament and cartilage connection not to the sternum but to the pair of ribs in front.

The lumbar spine

This region is equivalent to the loins. Six lumbar vertebrae continue from the thoracic part of spine. This complex area is characterized by the length and width of the transverse processes, which project horizontally to provide points of attachment for large, strong ligaments and muscle groups. They also provide protection for the organs that lie below.

This area of the spine is often described in conjunction with the thoracic vertebrae as the thoracolumbar spine. The spinous processes projecting upward from the top of the lumbar vertebrae are a similar length to the last few thoracic vertebrae.

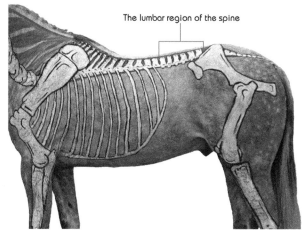

The lumbar region of the spine

The absence of ribs in the lumbar region makes this area appear weaker. The lumbar region transmits forces created at the hindend forward.

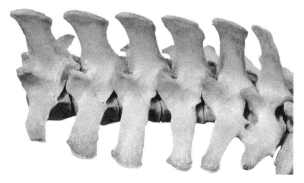

The lumbar vertebrae.

The next level - - - - - - -

The sacrum

This is a triangular bone comprising five vertebrae that fuse together by the time a horse is five years old. It provides a firm link between the hindquarters and the trunk. The sacrum attaches to the last lumbar vertebrae creating the lumbo-sacral junction. The first sacral vertebra has an enlarged transverse process, called the sacral wing. Together with the illiac wing of the pelvis this forms the sacroiliac joint (see page 28).

Ligaments of the back

The main ligaments support the back rather like a series of cables in a suspension bridge. They are:

- the supraspinous ligament, which lies on top of and attaches to each spinous process from the withers to the sacrum. As it moves away from the nuchal ligament it becomes more fibrous and less elastic. When stretched, the spine is arched slightly upwards. Its main function is to restrain the movements of the dorsal spines and keep the vertebrae in place thus giving the back support, strength and stability. When working efficiently in conjunction with the nuchal ligament, it enables the back muscles to contribute to propulsion as well as support and, together with the abdominal muscles, helps to lift the horse's back (see page 82)
- the ventral longitudinal ligament, which attaches to the underside of the vertebral bodies, and is only present from the fifth thoracic vertebra towards the tail. It is a powerful ligament that supports the thoracic, lumbar and sacral regions of the spine. It is stretched when the back is hollowed
- the interspinous ligament, which fills the gaps between the spinous processes, and provides further support and stability to the vertebrae. The fibres are attached diagonally so as not to interfere with flexion and extension of the back.

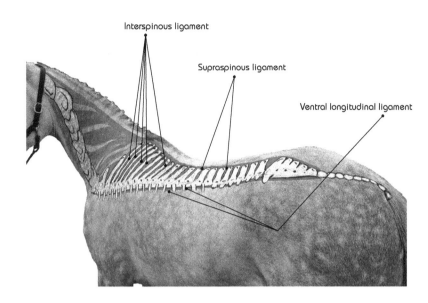

Interspinous ligament

Supraspinous ligament

Ventral longitudinal ligament

Musculature of the back

The main muscles involved in stabilizing the back are close to the spine and include the thoracis and lumborum sections of the multifidus muscle (see page 21). Further away from the vertebrae, the muscles become bulkier and more powerful. These muscles are responsible for gymnastic movement and for supporting the back. They are also involved in the forward transfer of movement created at the hind end.

They can be split into two groups:

- the main extensors of the back. These are the erector spinae group consisting of the iliocostals, longissimus dorsi (see page 20) and the spinalis thoracis muscles, which run along the top of the vertebrae and to either side of the spinous processes
- the main flexors of the back. These include the abdominal muscles, which consist of the internal and external abdominal oblique muscles, the transverse abdominal muscle and the rectus abdominis. These work together to hold the abdomen in place, to assist respiration by moving the ribs, and to support the correct positioning of the vertebral column. These muscles need to be strong to assist the back in supporting the weight of the rider.

SUMMARY

- **The horse's back consists of 18 thoracic and 6 lumbar vertebrae.**
- **There is little movement between these vertebrae.**
- **Strong ligaments support the back.**
- **The muscles that extend the back are situated above the vertebral bodies and include the longissimus dorsi muscle.**
- **Muscles that flex the back include the abdominal muscles.**

THE LUMBO-SACRAL JUNCTION, PELVIS AND THE SACROILIAC JOINT

This is an anatomically complex area. It is the only part of the skeleton where the axial and appendicular parts are in direct contact with one another via the sacroiliac joint.

The lumbo-sacral junction

The lumbo-sacral junction is the point at which the sixth lumbar and first sacral vertebra meet. This is a hinge joint. Approximately 20 degrees of flexion makes this the most flexible part of the spine after the neck and tail. This allows the horse to round his back and tilt his pelvis during canter and gallop (see pages 94–95 and 96–97). There is no sideways flexion or rotation here. For the horse to move well it is important that this joint is not impeded in any way.

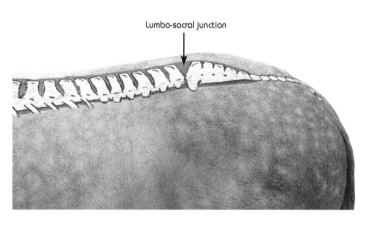

Lumbo-sacral junction

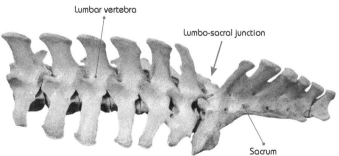

Lumbar vertebra

Lumbo-sacral junction

Sacrum

The angles of the spinous processes change at the lumbo-sacral junction. This can often be felt as a wider gap between the spinous processes.

The next level

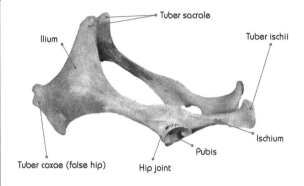

Tuber sacrale

Ilium

Tuber ischii

Ischium

Pubis

Tuber coxae (false hip)

Hip joint

The sacroiliac joint

The hind limb is attached to the sacrum at the sacroiliac joint where the wing of the ilium attaches to the large transverse process of the first sacral vertebra. This combined synovial and ligamentary joint has negligible movement and is held in place by very strong ventral, dorsal and sacroiliac ligaments.

The Pelvis

Each side of the pelvis consists of the three fused bones, the ilium, ischium and pubis.

The **ilium** is the largest pelvic bone. The outer edge of the ilium, the tuber coxae, can be felt and is known as the false hip. This is misleading as the actual hip joint is situated much further back. The top of the ilium is known as the tuber sacrale and forms the highest point of the rump, the jumper's bump. This is more prominent in lean horses. The more angled the pelvis, the more prominent the 'bump'. The wing of the ilium attaches to the sacrum at the sacroiliac joint.

The **ischium** is the rear of the pelvis, the end of which is the tuber ischii, this forms the point of buttock.

The **pubis** forms the pelvic floor which provides an extensive area for attachment of the abdominal muscles, which are crucial in lifting the back and tilting the pelvis.

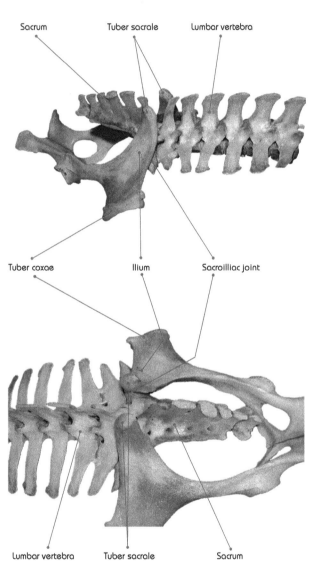

Sacrum

Tuber sacrale

Lumbar vertebra

Tuber coxae

Ilium

Sacroilliac joint

Lumbar vertebra

Tuber sacrale

Sacrum

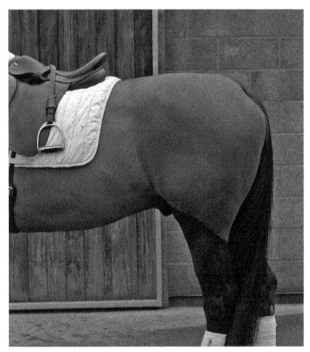

The angle of the pelvis and prominence of tuber sacrale determine conformation of this area. This horse has virtually no jumper's bump!

Muscles in this area

The main support and flexors of this area is the iliopsoas group. The muscles attach from the underside of the lumbar vertebrae and insert into the underside and inside of the pelvis and the inside of the top of the femur. As well as supporting the lumbar vertebrae and the sacroiliac, lumbo-sacral and hip joints, they help create flexion and rotate the hip.

The main extensor muscle of this area is the gluteal medius muscle (see page 32). This attaches into the thoraco-lumbar fascia in the lumbar region and inserts into the pelvis, hip and femur. As well as creating propulsion and being implicated in retraction of the hind limb, this muscle extends and supports the lumbo-sacral junction and the sacroiliac and hip joints, and transfers power from the hamstrings to the lumbar spine.

SUMMARY

- This is an anatomically complex area.
- The lumbo-sacral junction is the point at which the lumbar and sacral vertebrae meet.
- The lumbo-sacral junction is a hinge joint and after the neck and tail it is the most flexible part of the spine.
- The sacroiliac joint is the point at which the hind limb attaches to the spine.

The iliopsoas muscle group, which attaches from the underside of the lumbar vertebrae and the underside and inside of the pelvis, is so deep within the horse that it can only be felt by a vet through rectal examination.

FROM HIP TO HOCK

The function of the limbs, collectively referred to as the appendicular skeleton is to support the horse's weight, to propel him forwards, and also to help maintain his balance.

The hip joint and associated structures

The hip joint is situated deep within the hindquarter muscles. It must not be confused with the false hip (see page 28), the bony protrusion on the side of the pelvis.

The hip joint is the point at which the hind limb attaches to the pelvis. The ball-shaped head of the femur fits into the acetabulum, the cup-shaped cavity formed by the junction of the ilium, ischium and pubic bones. It is supported and stabilized by a fibro-cartilaginous ring and strong ligaments. As a ball and socket joint, the hip has a complete range of movement restricted only by the accessory ligament, which limits the leg moving up and away from the body.

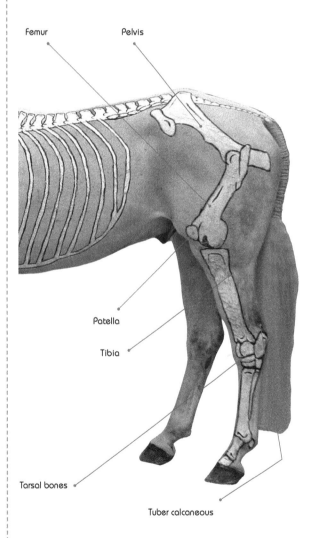

Femur

Pelvis

Patella

Tibia

Tarsal bones

Tuber calcaneous

The hind legs are the power house of the horse, reflected in the anatomy and the sheer size of the bones.

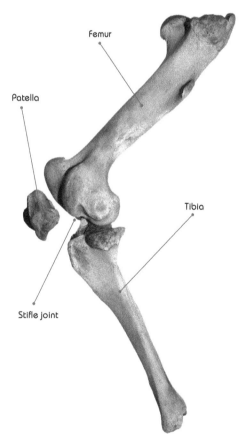

Femur

Patella

Tibia

Stifle joint

Upper limb bones from the right leg.

Tuber coxae (false hip)   Hip joint

The position of the hip can best be seen when the leg is manually rotated.

Femur

This long bone, adapted for the attachment of the strong muscles of the hindquarters, lies between the hip and the hinge joint of the stifle. It is one of the strongest and heaviest bones in the horse's body. At the base a groove lined with hyaline cartilage allows the patella, equivalent to our knee cap, to slide up and down.

Stifle joint

Equivalent to the human knee, the stifle joint forms the hinge between the femur and tibia. Concussion is absorbed through fibro-cartilaginous pads within the ligaments. The cruciate ligaments and collateral ligaments prevent overextension. The patella, situated at the front of the stifle, adds strength to tendons and fascia where they change direction.

Tibia and fibula

The tibia lies between the stifle and hock. Its main function is to provide an area for muscle and ligament attachment, the most important being the deep digital flexor tendon. The fibula is reduced and often absent in horses.

The hock

Made up of three rows of tarsal bones, the hock is a hinge joint equivalent to our ankle. The achilles tendon inserts into the tuber calcaneus. This bony prominence is called the point of hock and is equivalent to our heel. A complex arrangement of muscles, ligaments and tendons, enables the hock to work quickly and rhythmically. The hock and stifle work synchronously via the reciprocal system, see page 47. The hock absorbs concussion and withstands the propulsive forces generated within the hind limb.

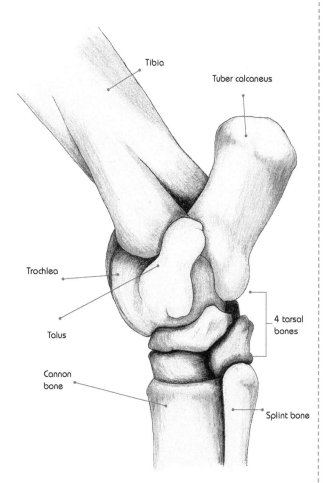

Tibia

Tuber calcaneus

Trochlea

Talus

Cannon bone

4 tarsal bones

Splint bone

The hock joint.

The next level

The muscles

The main driving force of the horse is provided by the muscles of the hindquarters and upper hind limb.

The **gluteals** are the muscles that give the hindquarters their powerful rounded appearance. They provide forward propulsion and strength. They lie on top of and behind the hip joint and can have a cross-section of up to 25–30cm (10–12in). There are three parts to the gluteals: the gluteal superficialis is mainly responsible for flexing the hip, the gluteal medius, which is the biggest of the group, is mainly responsible for hip extension, and the deep gluteal (gluteal profundus) is mainly responsible for abducting the thigh.

The **hamstrings** run down the back of the hind leg from the sacrum, the first few tail vertebrae, and the pelvis. They merge to become the achilles tendon attaching into the point of hock. The hamstring group is made up of the biceps femoris, semi-tendinosus and semi-membranosus. They play a major role in propelling the horse forward. They extend and stabilize the hip joint, extend and flex the hock and stifle, and allow the limbs to adduct and abduct.

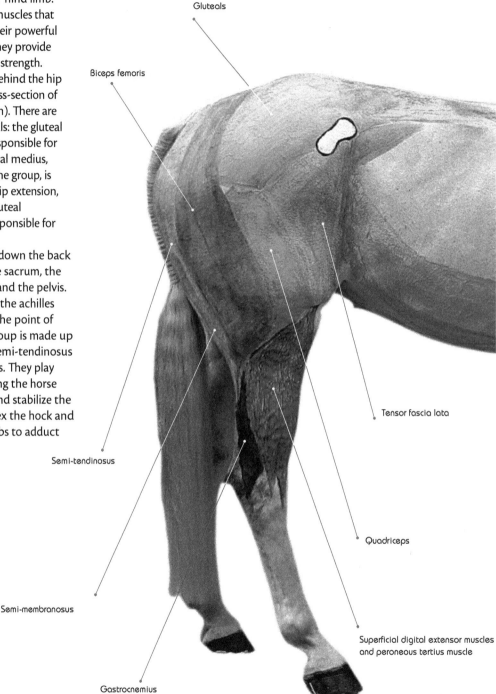

Gluteals

Biceps femoris

Tensor fascia lata

Semi-tendinosus

Quadriceps

Semi-membranosus

Superficial digital extensor muscles and peroneous tertius muscle

Gastrocnemius

Tensor fascia lata
muscle

When the tail is pulled to one side the tensor fascia lata muscle can clearly be seen.

The **tensor fascia lata** is the main hip flexor and lies in front of the hip. It is part of a group of muscles that acts in opposition to the gluteals and hamstrings. This muscle creates the shape of the flank from the false hip to the stifle. In conjunction with superficial gluteal and quadriceps femoris muscle, the tensor fascia lata extends the stifle and helps to bring the limb forward.

The **quadriceps muscles** lie in front of the stifle joint and with the main bulk of the muscle above the femur. They are the main extensors of the stifle. They also stabilize the joint during weight bearing phases of a stride.

The **gastrocnemius muscle**, equivalent to our calf muscle, together with other extensor muscles, inserts into the tuber calcaneus or point of hock.

The flexors of the hock lie in front of the joint and include the peroneous tertius muscle and the superficial digital flexor muscles. These muscles form the gaskin, the muscular region between the stifle and the hock.

SUMMARY

- The hindquarters are the powerhouse of the horse.
- The hip joint is the point at which the hind leg joins on to the pelvis.
- The position of the true hip must not be confused with that of the false hip.
- The muscles of the hindquarters can be up to 30cm (12in) in depth.

FROM SCAPULA TO KNEE

Whereas the hind limbs are the powerhouse of the horse, the forelimbs provide support, bearing approximately 60 per cent of a horse's body weight. They also aid balance and steering.

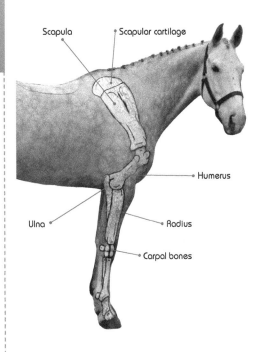

the first eight thoracic vertebrae. When a rider checks his diagonal, he is looking at the top of this cartilaginous extension. The spine of the scapula provides extra area for muscle attachment and can be felt under the skin.

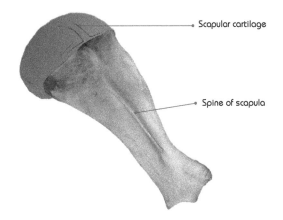

The main features of the scapula are the spine and the scapular cartilage, which is often mistaken for bone. Both features increase the area available for muscle attachment.

Thoracic sling

The horse has no collarbone. The limbs are connected to the body by ligaments, fascia, and a powerful set of postural muscles, which stabilize the shoulder and elbow and attach the scapula to the withers, spine and ribs. These soft tissue elements are collectively known as the thoracic sling. The sling enables the scapulae to glide over the ribs and trunk and allows the body to move freely between the scapulae and to roll into a turn at speed. This is important for balance. It also allows adduction and abduction of the front limbs, giving the body the capacity to move both forward and sideways at the same time (see pages 54–55).

The scapula

This large, triangular, flat bone, which partly covers the last cervical vertebra, the first seven thoracic vertebrae and the heads of the ribs that articulate with them, is ideally orientated at about 45 degrees. The smooth, slightly concave inner side of the scapula enables it to slide over the ribs as well as providing traction for the muscles and ligaments of the thoracic sling. The scapula is extended dorsally by the scapular cartilage, which provides an attachment for the forelimb to the nuchal ligament and

The shoulder joint

This is a synovial ball and socket joint formed at the junction of the scapula and humerus. Unusually, there are no collateral ligaments in the shoulder. This role is taken over by the infraspinatus, suprapinatus and subscapularis muscles, which control the amount of sideways and rotational movement.

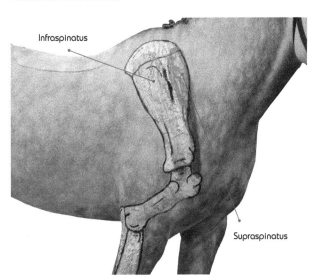

The humerus

The humerus, like the femur in the hind limb, is one of the strongest bones in the horse's body. It is angled to absorb shock and has various specialized indentations for the attachment of muscles and tendons. The greater tubercle, a bony prominence at the top end, creates the point of shoulder.

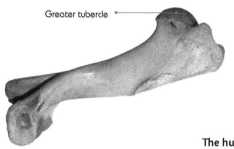

Greater tubercle

The humerus.

The elbow joint

As a synovial hinged joint between the humerus and radius and ulna, the elbow can only move in one plane. The olecranon process of the ulna provides attachment points for muscles that create leverage. This makes extension of the elbow joint, flexion of the shoulder, and movement of the forelimb more efficient.

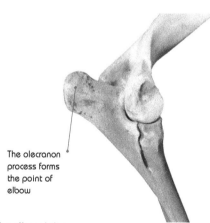

The olecranon process forms the point of elbow

The elbow joint.

The radius and ulna

These are equivalent to our lower arm. They are fused together in the horse for energy efficiency and to prevent twisting.

The knee

The term 'knee' is actually misleading as the horse's knee is equivalent to the human wrist. It comprises multiple, synovial hinged joints linking a series of seven or eight short, compact carpal bones arranged in two rows. The knee allows flexion, extension, and a minor amount of lateral movement to occur between the upper and lower forelimb. The important digital flexor tendons that control the lower limbs run in grooves behind the knee.

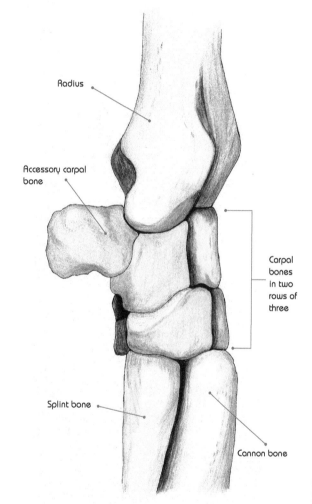

Radius

Accessory carpal bone

Carpal bones in two rows of three

Splint bone

Cannon bone

The knee joint.

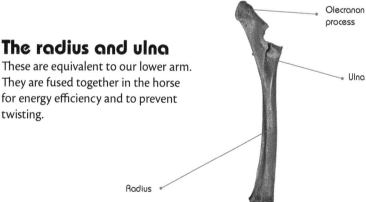

Olecranon process

Ulna

Radius

The next level

Main movers of the forelimb

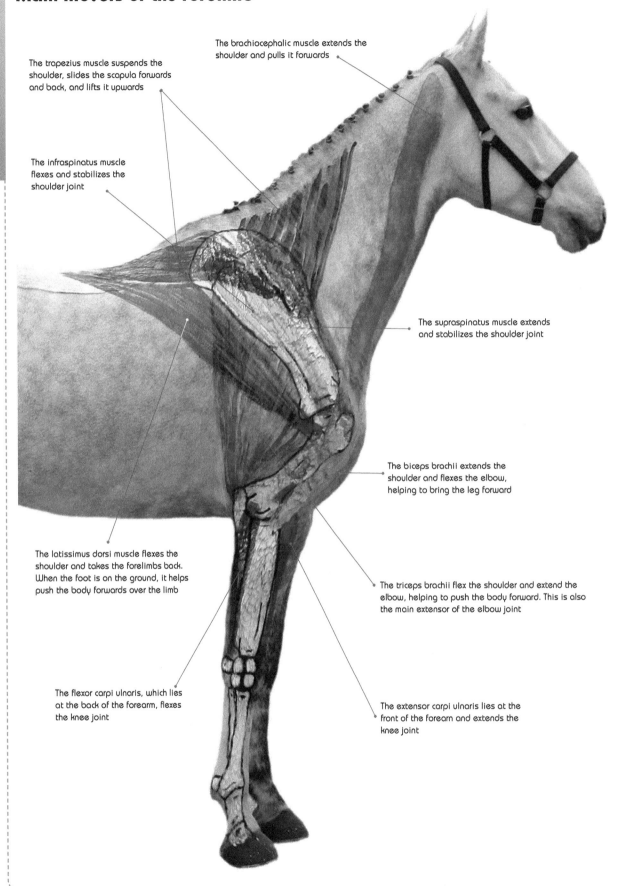

The brachiocephalic muscle extends the shoulder and pulls it forwards

The trapezius muscle suspends the shoulder, slides the scapula forwards and back, and lifts it upwards

The infraspinatus muscle flexes and stabilizes the shoulder joint

The supraspinatus muscle extends and stabilizes the shoulder joint

The biceps brachii extends the shoulder and flexes the elbow, helping to bring the leg forward

The latissimus dorsi muscle flexes the shoulder and takes the forelimbs back. When the foot is on the ground, it helps push the body forwards over the limb

The triceps brachii flex the shoulder and extend the elbow, helping to push the body forward. This is also the main extensor of the elbow joint

The flexor carpi ulnaris, which lies at the back of the forearm, flexes the knee joint

The extensor carpi ulnaris lies at the front of the forearm and extends the knee joint

BELOW THE KNEE

The lower limb has no muscles below the knee. This makes it light, allowing the horse to move at speed, and lowers demand for energy, improving endurance.

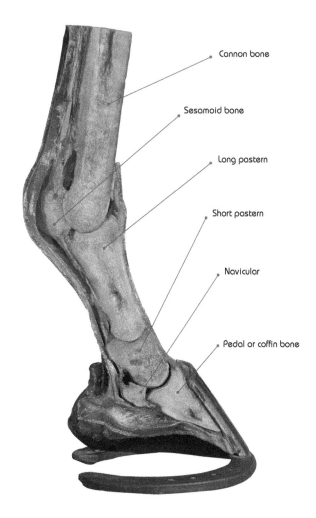

- Cannon bone
- Sesamoid bone
- Long pastern
- Short pastern
- Navicular
- Pedal or coffin bone

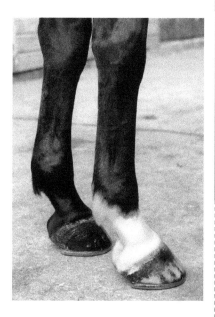

Bones of the lower limb

The bones below the knee consist of:
- the cannon bone, a slender, strong, weight-bearing long bone
- the two splint bones, these are the evolutionary equivalent to our index and ring finger. They come to an end about three quarters of the way down the cannon bone and the end can be felt as a small button
- the bones of the digital structures, these include the long and short pastern, two sesamoid bones, the navicular and pedal or coffin bone.

Together they form a complicated arrangement of joints and with cartilage, ligaments, blood vessels and nerves are the first bones of the leg to absorb concussion. The joints between the cannon and long pastern, the long and short pasterns and the short pastern and the pedal bone are hinge joints with a small amount of 'give' in the form of lateral movement and rotation. This allows the limb to cope when the foot is planted unexpectedly on an uneven surface causing the foot to twist.

Tendons of the lower limb

There are no muscles in the horse's leg below the knee. All movement of the pastern and foot is controlled by the muscles in the upper limbs via the tendons. This means that most of the movement in the lower limb occurs mechanically.

The joints of the lower limb are controlled via the tendons by the parent muscle situated above the knee. Where the tendons run over a joint, they are encased in a sheath which is lubricated with synovial fluid. This allows them to slide over one another and protects against friction. The tendons of the lower limbs are long and are subjected to enormous forces. They are a vital consideration in how the horse moves.

Tendons are either:
- flexors, which allow the joint to close, or bend inwards, toward the body, or
- extensors, which allow the joint to open or extend.

The extensor tendons lie at the front of the cannon bone with their muscles lying in front of the radius, whilst the flexor tendons run down the back of the limb with their muscles behind the radius and ulna.

The next level ------

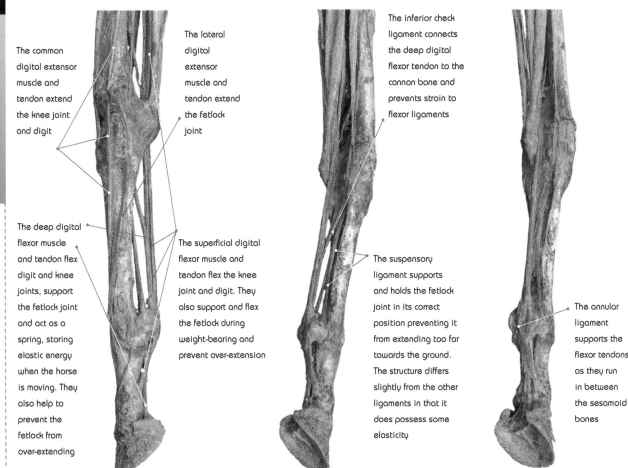

The common digital extensor muscle and tendon extend the knee joint and digit

The lateral digital extensor muscle and tendon extend the fetlock joint

The inferior check ligament connects the deep digital flexor tendon to the cannon bone and prevents strain to flexor ligaments

The deep digital flexor muscle and tendon flex digit and knee joints, support the fetlock joint and act as a spring, storing elastic energy when the horse is moving. They also help to prevent the fetlock from over-extending

The superficial digital flexor muscle and tendon flex the knee joint and digit. They also support and flex the fetlock during weight-bearing and prevent over-extension

The suspensory ligament supports and holds the fetlock joint in its correct position preventing it from extending too far towards the ground. The structure differs slightly from the other ligaments in that it does possess some elasticity

The annular ligament supports the flexor tendons as they run in between the sesamoid bones

Ligaments of the lower limb

The suspensory ligament is located between the deep digital flexor tendon and the cannon bone. It differs from other ligaments in that it is a modified muscle and so contains some muscular tissue. When the horse is weight bearing the suspensory ligament feels extremely hard and is often mistaken for the splint bone.

Horses also have check ligaments which prevent undue strain to the flexor tendons, connect some tendons to bones, and form part of the horse's stay mechanism (see pages 66–67).

The annular ligament is a broad band of ligamentous tissue that wraps around the back of the fetlock, holding the tendons in place and supporting the structures of the joint.

Below the knee and hock

The bones, tendons and ligaments in the lower leg are the same in the fore and in the hind leg, although the cannon bone tends to be longer and the pastern more upright in the hind leg.

NO FOOT, NO HORSE!

The foot is highly complex with enormous resilience and strength, allowing it to perform a variety of functions. A healthy hoof is crucial for soundness and, as most lameness comes from the foot, appreciating its anatomy can avoid problems and help in understanding when things go wrong.

The foot is encased by a keratin hoof, which grows from the coronet band that is situated directly above the hoof wall, protected by a thick layer of skin and hair. The darker band at the top of the hoof is the peripole, a special membrane that controls the amount of moisture in the foot. The wall, bars, and frog are the weight-bearing structures. These expand and contract with each step as weight is transferred from one foot to the next. The bones of the foot are held together by ligaments.

The main functions of the hoof are to:
• provide a weight-bearing surface not easily worn away
• protect the sensitive internal structures of the foot
• maintain moisture in the foot
• provide grip
• act as a shock absorber.

Inside the hoof

Perforations in the pedal bone help to reduce its weight.

The lower portion of the short pastern extends into the hoof capsule. The pedal bone provides the shape and rigidity required to bear weight. The navicular bone, situated just behind the pedal bone and in front of the bulbs acts as a pulley over which runs the deep digital flexor tendon, which is responsible for flexion of the foot. The hoof also contains cartilage, blood vessels and nerves. Sensitive laminae provide the main area of blood circulation within the foot and attach the hoof to the pedal bone.

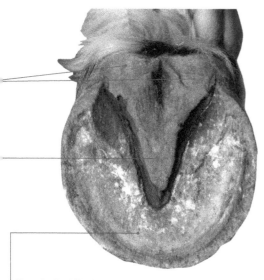

The sole should be firm, uniform in texture, and slightly concave. The softer fibrous white line joins the sole to form the inner layer of the wall

Spongy flexible frog is designed to weight-bear, but also acts like a pump, moving the blood back up the leg towards the heart

Bulbs of the heel are important in shock absorption

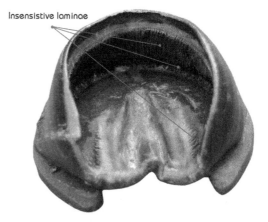

Insensistive laminae

Fast facts for feet!

• The hoof grows on average at 5mm per month.
• The fetlock is equivalent to our knuckles.
• There are two and a half bones within the foot!
• The horse walks on what is equivalent to the finger nail on our middle finger.
• The horse has no feeling in the outer sole.
• Horses shed the frog at least twice a year.
• The frog is equivalent to our finger tip.
• The pedal bone and the coffin bone are the same thing.
• Fore feet are rounder and slightly larger than hind as they bear more weight.

The next level

HOW THE HORSE MOVES

Before a human coach or trainer begins to train either an individual or team, he will have an understanding of how the human body works. This allows him to recognize the physical capability of their students and plan a training programme accordingly. The more we understand the physical make up of the horse the more accurate our expectations.

This chapter covers:

• how muscles create movement

• chain reaction!

• movement of the hind limb

• double trouble – the function of the lumbo-sacral and sacroiliac joints

• movement of the forelimb

• how the horse moves sideways

• tendons of the lower limb

• how the horse absorbs concussion

• how the horse bends

• the tail end

• how horses sleep standing up

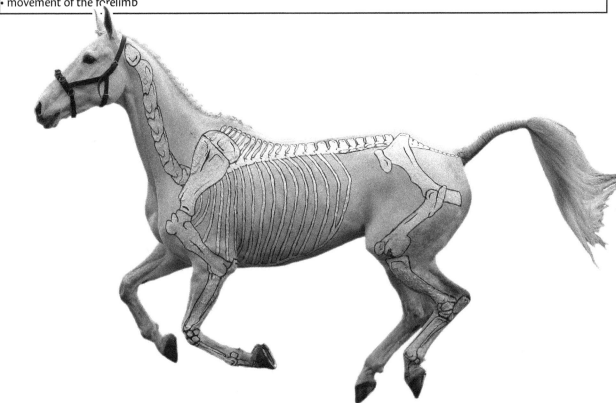

HOW MUSCLES CREATE MOVEMENT

Movement is created by the muscles pulling on the bones to operate the joints. They work across either one joint or several. The longissimus dorsi for example, crosses all the joints between the thoracic and lumbar vertebrae.

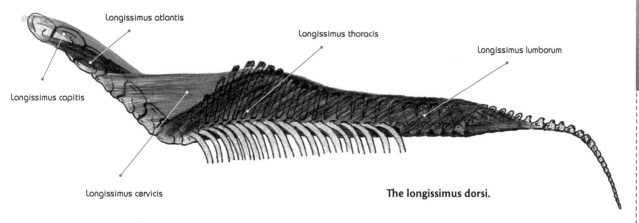

Longissimus atlantis

Longissimus thoracis

Longissimus lumborum

Longissimus capitis

Longissimus cervicis

The longissimus dorsi.

Muscle action

Essentially there are two groups of muscles, those involved in movement have longer fibres, and those involved in posture are shorter.

Muscle fibre arrangement for movement.

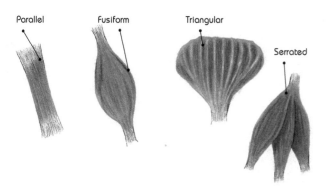

Parallel

Fusiform

Triangular

Serrated

Muscle fibre arrangement for posture and support.

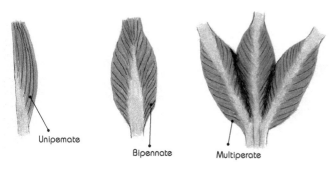

Unipennate

Bipennate

Multipennate

Muscle pairs

Different muscles can be employed to perform the same action, but basically they all function in the same way. Muscles work in pairs or groups to create movement. When one muscle contracts, its opposite number relaxes and vice versa.

Since most of the movement of the equine limb involves flexion or extension, the majority of muscles are either flexors or extensors.

The two groups of muscles are known as:
- **agonists**, which move the body part by shortening or contracting the muscle
- **antagonists**, which relax or stretch to allow movement to happen.

Types of contraction

Understanding muscle contraction enables the rider to train more sympathetically. Muscles are signalled to contract via nerve impulses. Relaxation occurs when the impulses cease.

Very simply as muscles work they perform either isotonic or isometric actions.

Isotonic action results in movement and can be subdivided into two categories, although all movement uses a mixture of both.
1. **Concentric** contraction is where a muscle shortens to create movement.
2. **Eccentric** contraction is where a muscle gradually lengthens to control movement, or support and stabilize joints. It also absorbs shock during abrupt movement, such as landing after a jump or coming to a sudden stop.

How the horse moves

The horse uses eccentric muscle contraction when coming to a sudden stop.

To maintain an outline the horse uses isometric muscle contraction. Supporting the head in a fixed position for any length of time causes tension to build up within the muscle.

Isometric action is where the muscle is working hard, but there is no change in the muscle length as it contracts to maintain a position. This type of muscle contraction can create fatigue and discomfort if the muscle is not appropriately conditioned.

Horses use isometric muscle contraction to brace and support themselves whilst travelling. This is why spending an hour in a horse box or trailer is equivalent to approximately 20 minutes trotting.

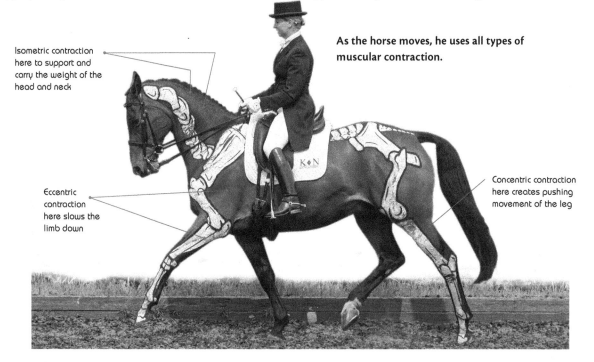

Isometric contraction here to support and carry the weight of the head and neck

Eccentric contraction here slows the limb down

As the horse moves, he uses all types of muscular contraction.

Concentric contraction here creates pushing movement of the leg

SUMMARY
- Muscles create movement by controlling the joints.
- They work in pairs and in groups.
- Opposing muscles are known as agonists and antagonists.
- Concentric muscular contraction produces movement by shortening the muscle.
- Eccentric contraction produces movement by lengthening the muscle.
- Isometric contraction causes the muscle to work but does not produce movement.

CHAIN REACTION!

Not only do muscles work in pairs and groups, they also work chains that combine to form a circle of muscles. This facilitates precise control and continuous flowing movement. Being aware of the concept of chains is useful when training the horse. There are two main muscle chains, the dorsal extensor chain and the ventral chain.

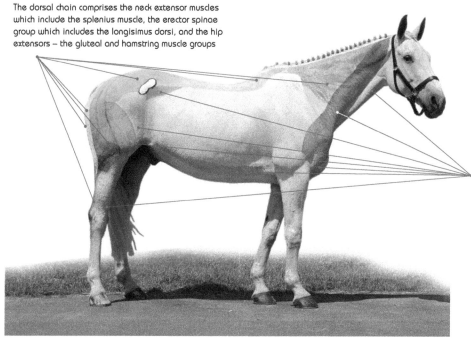

The dorsal chain comprises the neck extensor muscles which include the splenius muscle, the erector spinae group which includes the longisimus dorsi, and the hip extensors – the gluteal and hamstring muscle groups

The ventral chain comprises neck flexor muscles including the sternocephalic muscle, the pectorals, the flexors of the thoraco-lumbar spine and lumbosacral junction which include the abdominal muscles and the iliopsoas muscle, and the hip flexors including the tensor fascia lata muscle

The dorsal chain

This is sometimes called the extensor chain. These muscles, which make up the top line of the horse, are situated above the spine and behind the hip. This chain is involved in all forward movement, particularly cantering and jumping.

The dorsal or extensor chain of muscles is working hard as the horse extends his hip joint and pushes his body forwards.

The ventral chain

This is also known as the flexor chain. These muscles make up the bottom line and lie underneath the spine, in front of the hip, and include the abdominal muscles. As part of the 'core' muscles they have an important role to play in supporting and maintaining the correct posture of the back (see pages 74–75). They are also important in all movements requiring collection.

(see pages 74–75)

The flexor or ventral chain of muscle works hard as the hind leg is engaged.

TOP TIPS

Ridden exercises to improve the tone of the ventral chain muscles include:
• all transitions
• riding low and round in canter and trot
• gymnastic jumping over a small grid
• uphill work.

Trot pole work improves the tone of abdominal muscles.

Coordination of muscle chains

The dorsal and ventral muscle chains together form a circle of muscles that, when balanced, combine to create a state of equilibrium. Because there is often a greater focus on the top line muscles of the horse, the tone of the abdominal muscles is sometimes neglected. This can result in imbalance, which inhibits good movement.

Tension in any individual muscle in the chain may have a 'knock on' effect at any point throughout the chain. For example, if the longissimus dorsi is in spasm, it will affect the mechanics of the entire extensor chain and in turn inhibit the use of the flexor chain.

The importance of the abdominal muscles within the ventral chain cannot be overemphasized.

SUMMARY
• **Muscles work in chains.**
• **The dorsal muscles, above the spine and behind the hip create extension of the spine and hip, dip the back and raise the head and neck.**
• **The ventral muscles, below the spine and in front of the hip, create flexion of the spine and hip, helping to lift and support the back.**
• **The extensor and flexor chains of muscles must work in balance with each other to achieve correct movement.**
• **Restriction in one area can affect the entire chain.**

MOVEMENT OF THE HIND LIMB

Although it appears that the horse moves his forelimb first, movement is actually initiated in the hind limb. Once the hind limbs are flexed at the hip, stifle, hock, fetlock and pastern, energy is gathered and stored. During the stance phase the limbs are straightened, the body is pushed over the limb, and the horse is propelled forwards. Thus the horse can be likened to a rear wheel drive car in which the rear wheels provide the power. Understanding how the hind limb works can enable the rider to train horses more effectively.

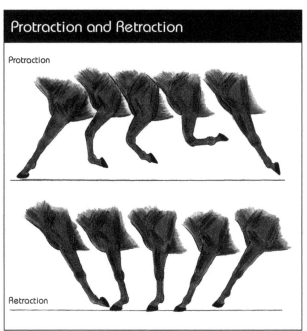

Movement is generated in the hindquarters, the power house of the horse.

Terminology of movement

The forward swing of the stride is known as **protraction** and the backward push is known as **retraction**. At the last moment of the **swing phase**, just before the foot makes contact with the ground, it goes into retraction in order to reduce the speed at which the limb makes contact with the ground. The part of the stride when the hoof is in contact with the ground is called the **stance phase**.

Protraction and Retraction

Protraction

Retraction

The pivotal point

The pivotal point is the point from which the leg swings. It is the uppermost joint involved in movement. In walk and trot, the hind leg swings from the hip joint. In canter and gallop the pivotal point moves up to the lumbo-sacral junction, although most of the movement still comes from the hip.

The pivotal point in trot (marked by a large red dot).

The pivotal point in canter (marked by a large red dot). Flexion and extension of the lumbo-sacral junction is easier when the hind legs are brought through together.

Protractor and retractor muscle chains

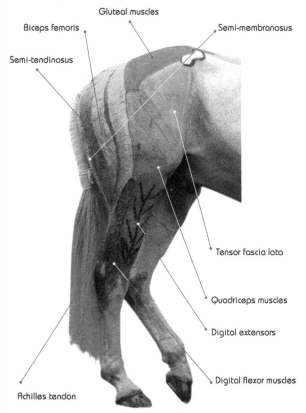

Semi-tendinosus

Biceps femoris

Gluteal muscles

Semi-membranosus

Tensor fascia lata

Quadriceps muscles

Digital extensors

Digital flexor muscles

Achilles tendon

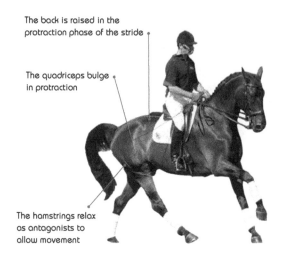

The back is raised in the protraction phase of the stride

The quadriceps bulge in protraction

The hamstrings relax as antagonists to allow movement

The muscles involved in protraction are painted on the horse in yellow, orange, pink and red. The muscles involved in retraction are painted in blue, green, turquoise and purple.

Protraction of the hind limb is initiated in the hip and carries the femur, stifle and hock forwards. The muscles running down the front of the femur, flex the leg, lift it, and bring it forward in protraction. The harder this muscle chain works, the further the horse reaches under himself, the greater the stride length, overtrack and height of step, all of which lead to more impressive steps.

All the antagonist muscles involved in retraction of the hind limb are elongated eccentrically during the protraction phase of the stride to ensure stability and smoothness of movement.

Retraction of the hind limb occurs once the leg is on the ground. The powerful muscles of the hindquarters straighten the hind leg and propel the body forward over it. The harder the leg pushes in retraction, the more power is created and the faster or higher the horse will go. As the leg pushes off ground, the pelvis straightens and the hip, stifle and hock joints extend. This means that the energy created is transmitted more efficiently to the back compared to if the joints were flexed. Energy is then transmitted forward along the dorsal muscle chain.

The muscles that bring the horse's leg backwards in retraction are at the back of the leg and include:
• the gluteals, which extend the hip and sacroiliac joint
• the hamstring group, comprising the biceps femoris, semi-tendinosus and semi-membranosus, which extend the hip and hock
• the gastrocnemius, which extends the hock
• the superficial digital flexor muscle and tendon, which flex the hock and joints of the lower limb.

All the antagonistic muscles involved in the protraction of the hind limb are elongated eccentrically to allow stability and smoothness of movement during retraction.

Muscles that bring the leg forward in protraction are at the front of the leg and include:

• the iliopsoas group, which flexes the hip and lumbosacral junction, tilting the pelvis
• the tensor fascia lata, which flexes the hip and extends the stifle
• the quadriceps, which extends the stifle
• the peroneous tertius, which flexes the hock when the stifle is flexed
• the long digital extensor muscle and tendon, which flex the hock and joints of the lower limbs
• the lateral digital extensor muscle and tendon, which flex the hock and joints of the lower limbs.

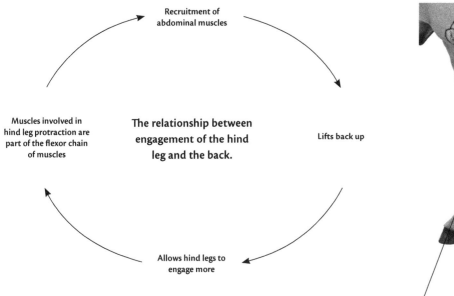

The relationship between engagement of the hind leg and the back.

Recruitment of abdominal muscles

Lifts back up

Allows hind legs to engage more

Muscles involved in hind leg protraction are part of the flexor chain of muscles

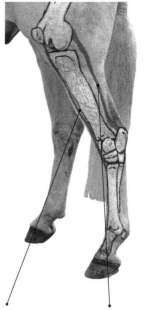

Peroneus tertius muscle

Superficial digital flexor tendon

The reciprocal system

A specialized arrangement of muscles and ligaments cause the stifle and hock to move in tandem. This means that when the stifle is flexed so is the hock and when the stifle is extended likewise so is the hock.

As they work in opposition to each other, it is the composition of the peroneal tertius and the superficial digital flexor muscles with a high proportion of connective tissue, but lower proportion of elastic muscle fibres, that causes them work as ligaments rather than muscles. This moves the joints in tandem.

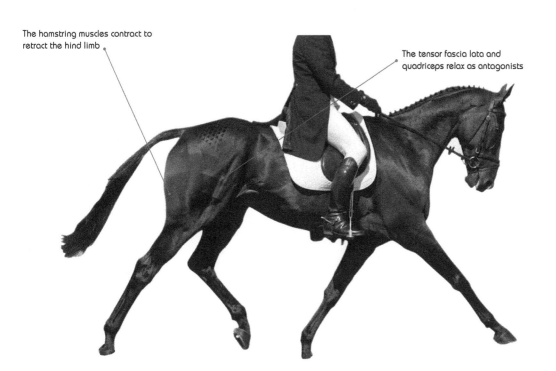

The hamstring muscles contract to retract the hind limb

The tensor fascia lata and quadriceps relax as antagonists

DOUBLE TROUBLE –
THE FUNCTION OF THE LUMBO-SACRAL AND SACROILIAC JOINTS

This is an anatomically complex, vulnerable region located just behind the saddle. The lumbo-sacral junction is the connection between the lumbar and sacral vertebrae and the sacroiliac joint is the point at which the pelvis is attached to the spine (see page 28).

Anatomy revisited

To all intents and purposes there is no movement at the sacroiliac joint. Movement of the pelvis comes as a result of a small amount of the flexion and extension (20 degrees maximum) of the hinged lumbo-sacral junction. The area is stabilized by strong muscular and ligamental attachments, which can be prone to strain. Horses with long backs and weak hindquarters are particularly susceptible. The further forward the lumbo-sacral junction is positioned, the less strain there is on the horse's back both in carrying the weight of the rider and in terms of maximum engagement.

It is the complexity of the anatomy, coupled with the fact that this part of the spine transmits the power and energy generated in the hind limb forwards as well as playing a role in absorbing concussion, that makes it such a hot spot for strains and sprains. Achieving maximum stability and flexibility in this area is the key for the horse to succeed as an athlete.

Relevance to movement

The lumbo-sacral junction has an important role to play in movement.

Canter and gallop – there is only minimal movement in the hinge joint of the lumbo-sacral junction in walk or trot. During the suspension phase of canter and gallop, both hind limbs come forward simultaneously ready to engage

Flexion of the lumbo-sacral junction allows greater engagement of the hind quarters in canter and helps to raise the back.

The lumbo-sacral junction extends to allow the hind legs to reach far out behind the body in canter and gallop.

the hindquarters. At this point flexion of the lumbo-sacral junction tilts the pelvis, allowing the hind legs to come further under the body and increase engagement. It also brings the hocks further under and contributes to lightening the forehand.

Jumping – in the last stride before a jump and at take off, the pelvis tilts and tucks under. The hocks and stifle flex, and the haunches lower, ready for the horse to launch himself upward (see pages 102–103).

Advanced dressage movements – in high level dressage – where the hind quarters are required to carry more weight behind and the horse must come up through the back and shoulders. There is increased flexion of the lumbo-sacral junction, as well as in the hips, stifles and hocks. This is accentuated in any movement requiring greater levels of collection, for example, piaffe, passage and canter pirouette.

In movements that require high levels of collection, the lumbo-sacral junction assumes a more flexed position, tilting the pelvis and helping to engage the hindquarters and shorten the frame.

Western riding – flexion of the lumbo-sacral junction can really be seen in the sliding western halt where movement in this area is taken to the extreme.

In barrel racing, because of the turning and twisting aspect involved in the sport, there is increased lateral and rotational strain in the sacroiliac area.

When a horse stops suddenly, the lumbo-sacral joint is put under strain and the short, fibrous connective tissue stabilizing the area around the pelvis and sacrum can tear.

Overextension – in cases of extreme, uncontrolled or repeated flexion and extension of the lumbo-sacral junction, the short ligaments connecting the sacrum and pelvis are under strain. This may lead to sacroiliac problems. Race or rodeo horses that skid and 'sit down' behind or horses that fall may suffer damage in this area.

SUMMARY

- The lumbo-sacral and sacroiliac area is a complex and vulnerable region.
- Its importance in transferring energy forward and absorbing concussion makes it a hot spot for strains and sprains.
- There is negligible movement at the sacroiliac joint.
- Flexion of the lumbo-sacral junction allows the pelvis to tilt and further tuck the hindquarters under thus increasing the range of movement.
- Sudden over-flexion or over-extension can lead to injury.

MOVEMENT OF THE FORELIMB

As the hind limbs provide engine power, the forelimbs provide the steering mechanism. They also absorb concussion and support the weight of the thorax. Together with the head and neck this accounts for about 60 per cent of body weight, which explains why the horse is naturally on the forehand. The bones of the forelimb are generally shorter and straighter than those of the pelvic limb.

The forelimbs are involved in turning, maintaining balance, braking and controlling power, which is generated by the hind limbs.

The muscles involved in protraction are painted in yellow, orange and pink while the muscles involved in retraction are painted in green, blue and turquoise. Notice that all of the muscles involved in retraction are down the back of the leg, and all of the muscles involved in protraction are down the front of the leg, with the exception of the trapezius muscle.

Protraction and retraction of the forelimb

Initiated in the shoulder, **protraction** carries the humerus, radius and ulna forwards. In the first part of the phase the joints are flexed and in the later part of protraction, they unfold and extend ready for ground contact. During protraction, the antagonistic muscles involved in retraction of the forelimb are elongated eccentrically (see page 41) to ensure stability and smoothness of movement.

The muscles that bring the leg forward in protraction include:
• the brachiocephalicus, which pulls the shoulder forwards
• the supraspinatus, which extends the shoulder joint
• the brachialis, which extends the shoulder joint and flexes the elbow
• the biceps brachii, which flexes the elbow joint
• the extensor carpi radialis, which extends the knee joint
• the common and lateral digital extensor muscles and tendons, which extend the knee and lower limb

• the thoracic portion of the trapezius muscle, which pulls the upper back of the scapula up and back.

When the hoof touches the ground, the muscles down the back of the leg and especially the latissimus dorsi, which runs from the shoulder area to the back, begin to pull the limb back in **retraction**. All the antagonistic muscles involved in the protraction of the forelimb are elongated eccentrically to allow stability and smoothness of movement during retraction.

How the horse moves

The muscles that bring the leg backwards during the retraction phase of the stride are:

- the latissimus dorsi, which pulls the shoulder and humerus backwards
- the infraspinatus and deltoid, which flex the shoulder joint
- the triceps brachii, which flex the shoulder and extend the elbow joint
- the tensor fascia antibrachii, which extends the elbow joint
- the flexor carpi radialis, which flexes the knee joint
- the superficial and deep digital flexor muscles and tendons which flex the knee and lower leg
- the cervical part of the trapezius muscle, which pulls the upper front of the scapula up and forwards.

The pivotal point

The forelimb is not attached to the rest of the body by bone, so it is unlike the hind limb in that there is no fixed pivotal point. Instead, the thoracic sling muscles allow the scapula to rotate via a gliding pivotal point, which is approximately two thirds of the way up the scapula. This facilitates extended movement and greater reach.

The contribution of the scapula to movement

The movement of the scapula allows the horse to adduct and abduct. This is particularly useful in coping with

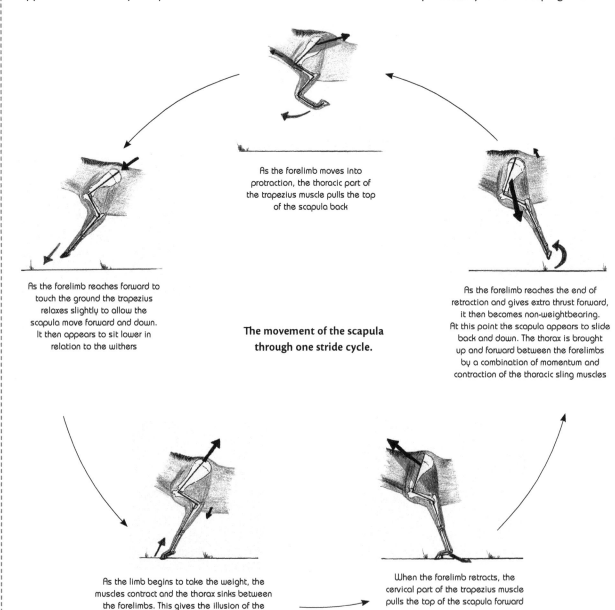

As the forelimb moves into protraction, the thoracic part of the trapezius muscle pulls the top of the scapula back

As the forelimb reaches forward to touch the ground the trapezius relaxes slightly to allow the scapula move forward and down. It then appears to sit lower in relation to the withers

The movement of the scapula through one stride cycle.

As the forelimb reaches the end of retraction and gives extra thrust forward, it then becomes non-weightbearing. At this point the scapula appears to slide back and down. The thorax is brought up and forward between the forelimbs by a combination of momentum and contraction of the thoracic sling muscles

As the limb begins to take the weight, the muscles contract and the thorax sinks between the forelimbs. This gives the illusion of the scapula sliding up in relation to the withers. This action also helps to absorb shock

When the forelimb retracts, the cervical part of the trapezius muscle pulls the top of the scapula forward

uneven ground and also when performing intricate dressage movements.

The angle at which the scapula lies also has important the implications for movement. The more angled the scapula, the greater the range of movement and the greater the ability of the forelimbs to fold when jumping.

A sloping shoulder.

An upright shoulder.

The point of tree should sit two finger-widths behind the back of the rigid scapular cartilage.

Saddles and the sliding scapula!

The sliding movement of the scapula should be taken into account when fitting a saddle. It is important to ensure the saddle does not pinch or restrict movement as discomfort will result in pain and poor performance.

Problems can be avoided by riding the horse in a correctly fitted saddle. A tree that is too narrow or 'pinches' may restrict scapula movement and cause pain resulting in short, hollow steps. It is important that saddle fit is assessed whilst the horse is being ridden. The fit of a jumping saddle should be assessed whilst the horse is jumping. The fit also needs to be checked at regular intervals.

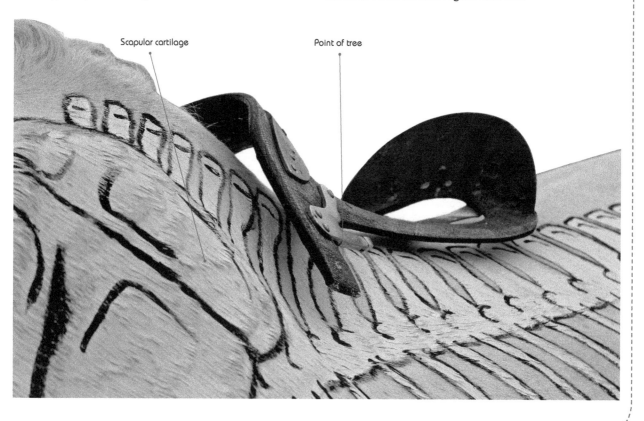

Scapular cartilage   Point of tree

HOW THE HORSE MOVES SIDEWAYS

During lateral movements, such as leg yielding, half pass, shoulder-in and travers, the horse is asked take his forelimbs or hind limbs across the centre of his body. In effect he is crossing over his legs. This is called **adduction**. When he steps out to the side, this is called **abduction**. These movements, useful to compensate for the rigidity of the spine, are seen in higher levels of dressage and are particularly useful for balance, bending and turning.

At a more basic level, sideways movements are useful for such manoeuvres as opening gates, for travelling across sloping ground and to put a leg out to the side to maintain balance.

Moving sideways is not a natural movement for the horse, although he can be trained to do so. In order to achieve this, he needs to be supple and stable through his musculature.

The primary role of the adductor and abductor muscles is to stabilize the legs and to prevent them from slipping out to the side.

Forelimbs

Sideways movement in forelimbs is made possible by the thoracic sling. This allows the legs to deviate from their alignment by letting the shoulder blade lift slightly in relation to the thorax. The trapezius and rhomboid muscles anchor the top of the shoulder blade whilst the leg abducts. The pectoral muscles, which run from the sternum to the forearm, allow the leg to adduct.

The thoracic sling allows abduction of the forelimb. The abductor muscles of the forelimb run down the outside of the leg and include the infraspinatus, supraspinatus and deltoid muscles.

The adductor muscles of the forelimb run down the inside of the leg and include the pectoral muscles

Biceps femoris   Gluteals

Muscles that are responsible for abduction of the hind limb include the gluteal and biceps femoris.

Hind limbs

Because the hip is a ball and socket joint which allows for a greater degree of rotation, the hind legs are able to move away from, or in and across the midline. Lifting the leg out to the side is not a natural movement for the horse and is generally only seen when the horse lifts his leg to scratch it with his teeth, kicks out to the side, is being shod, or a therapist manually rotates the hip joint. Sideways movement is limited by the ligaments around the hip joint. The range of movement forward and back is far greater than to either side.

TOP TIP

To move sideways demands practise and gentle strengthening of the unaccustomed muscles. To teach the horse to go sideways begin with a simple leg yield. This will recruit all the correct muscles, strengthen them, and teach him to step under.

The main adductor muscles of the hind limb run from the underside of the pelvis and insert into the inside of the femur and tibia.

SUMMARY

• Adduction occurs when the horse brings his leg towards the centre of his body.
• Abduction is when the horse moves his leg away from the centre of his body.
• The muscles responsible for adduction run down the inside of the leg.
• The muscles responsible for abduction run down the outside of the leg.
• The primary function of the adductor and abductor muscles is to support and stabilize the limbs.

TENDONS OF THE LOWER LIMB

The main function of the tendons is to transfer the energy created in the muscles above the knee to the lower limb. Each muscle and tendon work as one unit. Tendons can be:
- flexor tendons that flex the leg. They are put under greater stress than the extensors
- extensor tendons that extend the limb and bring it forward.

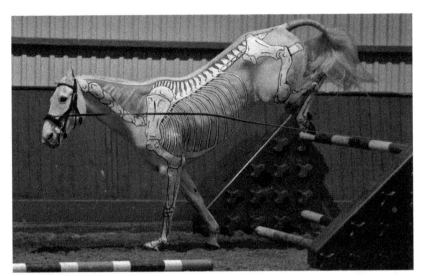

Extension of the fetlock joint occurs when one limb is required to support the entire weight of the horse.

Extension of the fetlock joint

Approximately one tonne of force is required to fully extend the fetlock joint in the horse. The forces are maximized in the faster paces, when landing after a jump, or during high levels of engagement.

Sudden acceleration or braking can also cause the fetlock to hyper-extend to such an extent that it brushes the ground. Racehorses sometimes wear fetlock protectors to prevent their fetlock joints from bruising.

When the fetlock is over extended, it is the deep and superficial digital flexor tendons and the suspensory ligament that support it. If the fetlock is repeatedly put under strain, injury is more likely to occur (see pages 120–121).

How the tendons support movement

As the horse begins to put weight on the leg, the suspensory ligament is the main support. As full weight is applied, the superficial and then the deep digital tendons come into play and take part of the load. If support for the deep digital flexor tendon after full weight bearing is either inadequate or delayed by circumstances, such as uneven ground, the superficial tendon and/or the suspensory ligament will be put under additional strain and are at risk of being damaged.

During the weight-bearing phase of the stride, it is the digital flexor tendons which, along with the suspensory ligament, support the lower joints – in particular the fetlock joint.

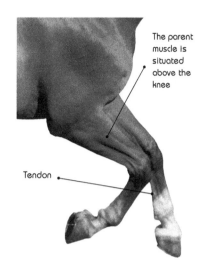

The parent muscle is situated above the knee

Tendon

Healthy tendons, as well as having the ability to bear extreme stretching forces, can also store energy and absorb minor overloads during exercise. Exceeding the limits of their ability to stretch can result in damage.

Stretch...

As the tendon is stretched in the early stance phase of the stride (see page 45), it stores elastic energy. This is rather like an extended spring.

...and recoil

When the weight is released later in the stance phase, the spring, in this case the superficial digital flexor tendon, recoils, releasing the energy. It is this action that acts as an energy saving mechanism for the parent muscle.

TOP TIP

Avoid hard rutted ground that can cause the fetlock to twist or over-extend, thus increasing the strain on the lower leg.

SUMMARY

- Tendons transfer the energy from the parent muscle above the knee to the lower limb .
- They have the ability to stretch and recoil.

HOW THE HORSE ABSORBS CONCUSSION

Concussion is the impact and jar of a horse's feet and legs upon the ground as they travel. The greater the forces, the further the concussion travels and the greater the effect on the tissues. It is a major factor in lameness.

The factors that affect concussion

Impact from different types of surface plays a large part in absorbing concussion. A hard, impacted surface with no 'give', such as roads, sun baked pasture in summer, or frozen ground in winter, can play havoc with the legs. When training, it is advisable to work on a surface that 'gives', that is neither too deep nor too hard.

Force is weight combined with speed and this creates a tremendous amount of concussion on a few square inches of hoof. The shorter the time that the foot is on the ground, the greater the force. For example, in canter, the foot is on the ground for half the length of time that it is in walk so concussion forces are greater and need to be absorbed in half the time.

Conformation is especially important in the front limbs because they are subject to greater concussion than the hind. Thus forelimb lameness is more prevalent and conformation faults more serious. If legs, joints and feet are strong, they can withstand greater concussive forces. The nearer the leg is to ideal conformation, the more easily it will cope. Horses with poor conformation have less chance of absorbing concussion effectively.

Shoeing protects the hooves and considerably limits the effects of concussion by spreading its effects. A good farrier will level each foot to allow optimum function of all the structures and to ensure the shoe addresses the ground on a level plane.

The trauma caused as a result of repeatedly hitting a hard surface and the constant wear and tear on bones, joints and ligaments over time may ultimately lead to damage.

The more forgiving the surface, the more easily concussion will be absorbed.

When a horse lands from a jump, the trailing forelimb has to absorb twice his body weight.

The structures that absorb concussion

The **foot**, frog, heel, sole and wall of the hoof expand as the foot takes the weight. Inside the hoof capsule, the circulating blood and the laminae also cushion impact.

The **pastern** joint absorbs most of the impact transmitted upward from the foot. A sloping pastern has more concussion-absorbing qualities than a short, steep pastern. The ideal angle is 45 degrees.

The **fetlock**, together with the sesamoid bones and its strong ligaments, has an important part to play in the absorption of concussion.

The **knee**, in which the carpal bones are separated by a layer of cartilage and synovial fluid, allow a small degree of movement and are designed to absorb concussion.

The **hock,** in conjunction with the stifle and hip joints, absorbs most concussion in the hind limb. There is less movement in the tarsal bones of the hock than in the carpal bones of the knee, but the permanent partial flexion of the hock also helps to absorb concussion.

Horse with upright pasterns.

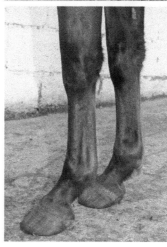

Horse with sloping pasterns.

How the horse moves

The fetlock extends due to the stretch in the suspensory ligament and the deep and superficial digital flexor tendons.

In the **shoulder and elbow**, the angle of the humerus in relation to the shoulder and elbow joints, ideally at about 60 degrees, acts rather like a suspension system. As the forelimb comes into contact with the ground, the joints flex to absorb energy.

In the **thoracic sling**, the muscular and ligamental attachments prevent jarring by allowing 'give' in the soft tissues, thus reducing 'jar' as the limbs hit the ground.

Muscles have an important role to play in dissipating the effects of concussion. If they are tense, more concussion will be taken by the joints putting them under additional strain. A healthy musculature ensures forces are distributed more evenly throughout the body.

In the **back and pelvis**, most of the concussion, which is not absorbed lower down the hind leg, is absorbed in the sacroiliac joint. Concussion especially in the hind limbs can contribute to pain in the sacroiliac and lumbar region.

TOP TIPS

- Exercise strengthens the body and its structures. Keeping the horse well conditioned, fit and lean will help to avoid concussive injuries.
- Supple, well-conditioned muscles are able to absorb concussion much more readily than tight restricted ones.
- Avoiding fast work and jumping on hard ground will significantly reduce concussion.
- Good farriery keeps feet in the best possible condition for absorbing impact shock.
- Reducing the amount of weight carried will limit the effects of concussion.

SUMMARY

- **Consider the surface.**
- **Speed x Force = Concussion.**
- **Concussive forces are mainly absorbed in the forelimbs**
- **The foot, fetlock, knee and hock are the major shock-absorbing structures.**
- **The nearer the leg is to ideal conformation, the better it will stand up to concussion.**

HOW THE HORSE BENDS

Although we often think about the horse bending from poll to tail, this does not actually happen evenly along the horse's length. This is because the flexibility of the spine varies along its length – the neck, for example, is more flexible than the lumbar region.

Lateral bend

This refers to the curvature of the horse's spine around the rider's inside leg on circles and corners. For example, when riding a 20m circle, the spine should be bent in such a way that it matches the ground track, the spine following the curve of the circle from poll to tail. The bend should be moderate and regular. It is harder for the horse to bend on a smaller circle. Bend is a desirable trait frequently referred to by trainers, required by dressage riders and necessary to maintain balance.

Difficulties in bend are related to the horse's anatomy. The neck is very flexible, the back and ribcage virtually rigid and then the tail is more flexible again. The thoracic spine, a more rigid part of the structure is further hampered by the saddle. The lumbar spine, by virtue of the way the vertebra articulate with each other and with the sacrum cannot bend sideways at all.

How the horse bends

The ability of a horse to bend is not only determined by the bones and joints; muscles and limb movement also play a part. A horse can bend in a number of ways.

By using his neck – most flexion occurs at the cervico-thoracic junction at the base of the neck. Excessive bend in the neck may cause the hindquarters to swing out.

By using his back – there is a very small amount of lateral flexion between the joints of the thoracolumbar vertebrae, the most being around the 12th and 13th. Flexion of these joints is stimulated by a reflex positioned beneath the rider's leg. When stimulated on one side, this reflex causes slight rotation of the ribs and flexion of the spine away from the pressure. When stimulated on both sides simultaneously, it causes the horse to lift his ribcage.

Riding a circle in perfect balance is one of the most difficult things for a horse to perform.

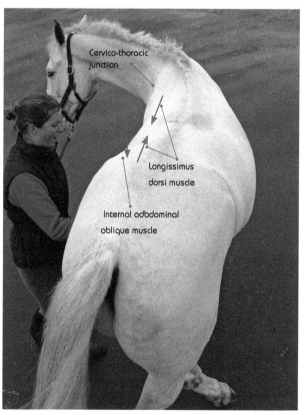

Cervico-thoracic junction

Longissimus dorsi muscle

Internal adbdominal oblique muscle

Much of the lateral flexion of the thoracolumbar spine comes from contraction of the longissimus dorsi muscle.

By engaging the muscles – one set of muscles contract to flex certain joints, or to bend the neck and ribcage. Meanwhile the antagonistic set of muscles (see page 41) stretch to allow the bend or flexion to occur. These muscles can be strengthened and made more supple by changing the bend so the muscles stretch and contract alternately.

Tension in the muscles can affect the ability to bend. For example, if the horse has stiff muscles on the right, he may find it harder to bend to the left and visa versa.

By moving the ribs – the ribs attach to the thoracic vertebrae via small synovial joints designed to allow the chest to expand for breathing. Movement here is limited to a few centimetres. A slight shift of position in one rib affects next in line, which results in a cumulative change along the length of the thoracic spine.

Movement in the synovial joints also allows the ribcage to rotate to one side. This can be seen clearly when the horse turns on a small circle (see arrow on picture to the right). As the horse steps through with the inside hind, the neck is flexed to the inside, the ribs on the inside compress and the outside ribs open.

By employing the tail – lateral flexion of the tail contributes to the illusion of bend.

By the sliding function of the scapula – as the shoulders work independently, one can slide more than the other. When the inside leg is placed on the ground, the outside shoulder rises, comes further forward and round, and thus contributes to the bend on a circle.

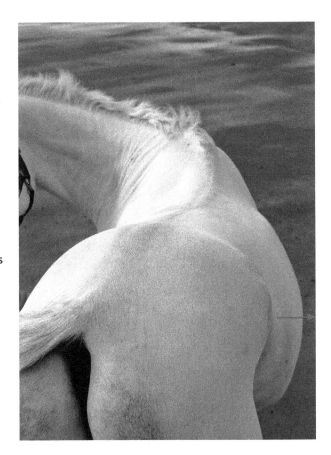

By the action of the thoracic sling – the suspension of the thoracic sling allows the thorax to rotate as well as move up, down, forwards and backwards within the confines of the bony pillars of the forelimbs.

How to feel movement or 'spring' in the ribs:

1. stand level with and facing the horse's flank
2. pull the tail towards you
3. gently push the ribs away.

Note:
Some horses do not like this movement!

By abduction and adduction – by adducting or abducting the limbs, both the hind legs and fore legs contribute to the bend. This is more pronounced as the size of the circle decreases. A stiff horse that finds it difficult to bend his spine, may swing his quarters out to the side or be reluctant to adduct his inside hind leg.

By leaning in – some horses may also lean in on turns to aid balance.

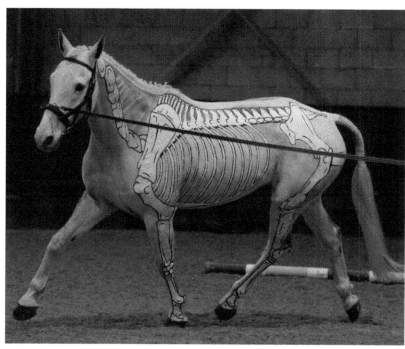

Adduction of the inside hind leg, can clearly be seen here.

The tighter the turn the more a horse leans in.

TOP TIPS

Any lateral work where the horse moves forwards and sideways simultaneously will increase bend.

- Ride circles in trot and canter, beginning at 20 metres and including both inward and outward spirals.
- Ride serpentines, beginning with three loops, then gradually increasing the number.
- Ride ever decreasing figures of eight.
- Introduce leg yield to encourage the horse to step under with the hind leg.
- Progress to shoulder in. Begin by achieving a good bend at walk before progressing to trot and then canter.

With all these exercises make sure the required level of bend is comfortably achieved before progressing to the next level.

THE TAIL END

The tail consists of eighteen to twenty-two caudal vertebrae, which are smaller and less complicated than other vertebrae of the spine, comprising simply of vertebral bodies. There is no spinal cord as this peters out in sacral vertebrae. Caudal vertebrae are linked by cartilaginous discs, which make the tail highly mobile.

Movement is controlled by the semi-tendinosus muscles, which extend over the rump to the vertebrae. Specific adjustments in curvature and posture of the tail are refined by bundles of muscle fibres surrounding the bones.

Functions

The tail is used for protection and communication.

It protects by:
- covering the anus and urethra
- providing a barrier against the elements. The coarse hairs at the top of the tail are ruffled when the horse stands with his back to inclement weather
- acting as a highly efficient fly swat!

It communicates:
- excitement, arousal, aggression or fear when held high and combined with high head carriage, high bouncing steps, and a long phase of suspension
- submission, ill health, tiredness or fear when drooping or clamped down in association with low head carriage
- irritation, pain, fear and resistance in the ridden horse by swishing. This is seen, particularly in dressage, as a sign of resistance but is not always the case. Some top dressage horses swish their tails and are perfectly submissive.

Movement

The tail is not generally considered to have any role in movement, however, as a string of vertebrae linked by muscle chains, ligaments and fascia, it can act as a balancing rod.

Horses sometimes flick their tails upwards as they flick their hind feet over a jump.

Tail flicking often accompanies exuberant behaviour.

Tail carriage

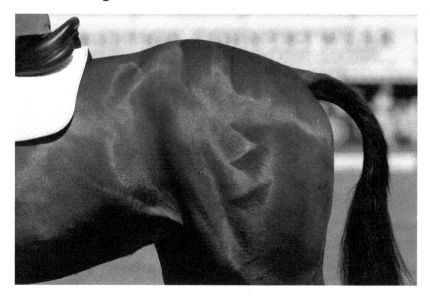

Ideally the horse should carry his tail well sprung. This is dependant on conformation and is an aesthetic consideration only.

As the tail is a continuation of the spine, linked by ligaments and muscles, it may have implications for tension further forward in the spinal column. Poor circulation in the tail makes it slow to heal in the event of injury.

Tail carriage can be a reflection of:
• pain or muscle spasm in the back. Tail clamping can occur in response to spasm in the intervertebral multifidus muscle, which extends into the tail
• misalignment or kinks due to congenital defect or injury. Scar tissue can be less elastic and can affect tail posture.

A clamped tail may be an indication of muscular tension either in the hindquarters or further forward in the back.

A tail held to the side may be an indication of crookedness, pain, or muscular tension further forward in the spine.

SUMMARY
• The main functions of the tail are protection and communication.

HOW HORSES SLEEP STANDING UP

Sleep patterns in horses

Horses sleep or doze in short bursts, most of which are spent standing up.

Research has shown the amount of sleep varies considerably between individuals, but horses actually need as little as two and a half hours of light sleep per day. They also need a couple of hours of deep sleep about once every forty-eight hours, which must be spent lying down.

Once down the rigidity of the spine makes it difficult for a horse to get up. This takes a considerable amount of muscular energy and is often accompanied by a grunt of effort.

Outside, horses sleep better in groups because some sleep while others stand guard. This behaviour emanates from the need to make a rapid exodus from predators.

Horses can sleep standing up because the stay apparatus in their legs allows them to relax their muscles and doze without falling down or expending much energy

The stay apparatus

This is a unique system of interlocking muscles, tendons and ligaments that allow the joints in the limbs to be 'locked' in position with minimal muscular effort. Once locked, the limbs become rigid, rather like the legs of a chair. Body weight is then suspended with little muscular effort. The arrangement is much the same in the fore and hind limbs.

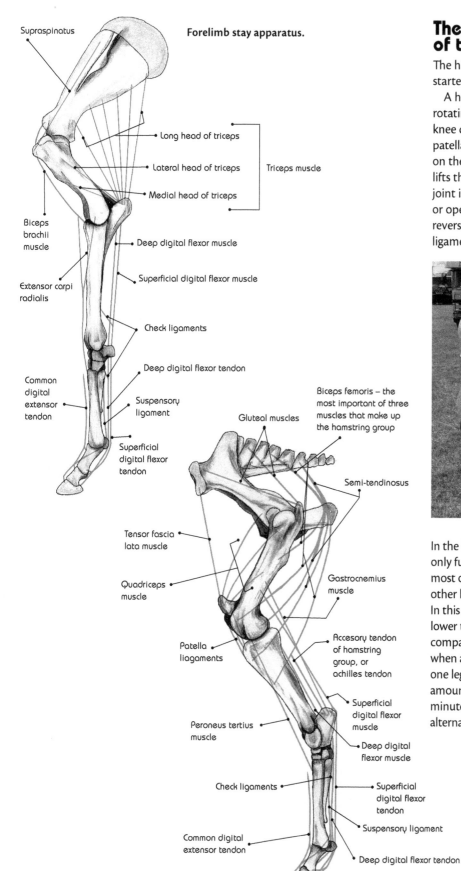

Supraspinatus

Forelimb stay apparatus.

Long head of triceps

Lateral head of triceps

Triceps muscle

Medial head of triceps

Biceps brachii muscle

Deep digital flexor muscle

Extensor carpi radialis

Superficial digital flexor muscle

Check ligaments

Deep digital flexor tendon

Common digital extensor tendon

Suspensory ligament

Superficial digital flexor tendon

Biceps femoris – the most important of three muscles that make up the hamstring group

Gluteal muscles

Semi-tendinosus

Tensor fascia lata muscle

Quadriceps muscle

Gastrocnemius muscle

Patella liagaments

Accesory tendon of hamstring group, or achilles tendon

Peroneus tertius muscle

Superficial digital flexor muscle

Deep digital flexor muscle

Check ligaments

Superficial digital flexor tendon

Common digital extensor tendon

Suspensory ligament

Deep digital flexor tendon

Hind limb stay apparatus.

The locking mechanism of the stifle

The hind leg stay apparatus is kick started by locking the stifle.

A horse locks the stifle by lifting and rotating the patella, equivalent to our knee cap, then hooking it with the patellar ligament over a protuberance on the femur. The quadriceps muscle lifts the patella. Once secured, the joint is then locked in an extended or open position. This can be quickly reversed by unhooking the patella ligament, thus releasing the stifle.

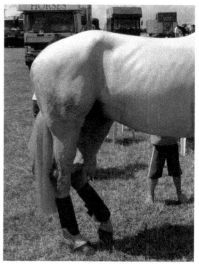

In the hind limb the stifle and hock are only fully locked when the horse puts most of its weight on one limb. The other leg rests on the tip of the hoof. In this position, the resting hip sags lower than the supporting one. This is comparable to a person's relaxed hip when all the body weight is put on the one leg. This does take a minimum amount of muscular effort so every few minutes the horse will shift its weight, alternately resting the other leg.

How the horse moves

THE WAY OF GOING –
AN ANATOMICAL PERSPECTIVE

Many training mistakes could be avoided if riders acquired an understanding of how the horse functions and learned to recognize and respect the horse's physical and physiological make up. This section aims to help in understanding some of these things.

This chapter covers:

• flexion at the poll

• the function of the nuchal ligament

• spinal posture

• how positioning of the head and neck affects the way of going

• how the horse sees

• core stability

• impulsion

• how the horse carries the weight of the rider

• maintaining straightness

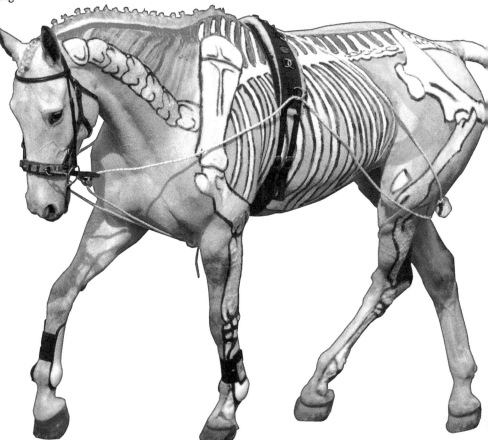

FLEXION AT THE POLL

Flexion is a compliant and athletic bending at the poll that indicates acceptance of the bit. The horse should move forward willingly while holding his nose in a vertical plane. Flexion is only achieved if the horse is ridden softly.

Why flex?

Both extension and over-flexion are undesirable and inhibit correct movement. Flexion at the poll is important in the ridden horse because anatomically it allows the horse to develop correct posture, alignment and straightness.

Understanding the terminology

Longitudinal flexion is where the poll area softens and the horse accepts the bit, allowing the nose to come nearer the vertical.

Lateral flexion is where the horse turns his head to the left or right. The nose will remain vertical.

Rotation is where the horse tilts his head in a 'no' type shake.

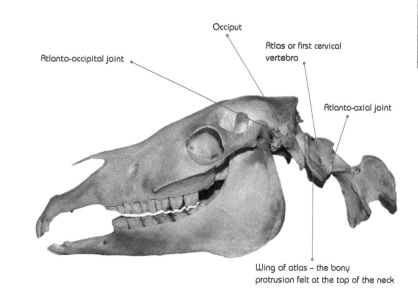

Occiput

Atlas or first cervical vertebra

Atlanto-occipital joint

Atlanto-axial joint

Wing of atlas – the bony protrusion felt at the top of the neck

A closer look at anatomy

Flexion occurs at a joint. It is the opposite of extension. Flexion at the poll refers to movement between the skull and first cervical vertebrae.

Between the skull (or occiput) and the atlas (the first cervical vertebrae) is the atlanto-occipital joint. This is a hinge joint that allows vertical or nodding type movement. When the nose is vertical, and the atlanto-occipital is flexed, it is also possible to have some lateral flexion at this joint. If the horse pokes his nose out forward and upwards, the joint locks laterally inhibiting lateral flexion at the poll.

When the atlanto-occipital junction is extended, no lateral flexion can be achieved. This means that if the horse's nose is not vertical, he cannot turn his head to the side from the poll.

The way of going

A good exercise to ensure the horse is longitudinally submissive at the poll is to ask for slight lateral flexion to the inside or outside. Not until he is longitudinally submissive will he be able to achieve true lateral flexion at the poll.

Lateral flexion and submission at the poll can only be achieved when there is longitudinal submission. In other words, the horse can only turn his head to the side when he is relaxed into the contact.

The joint between the first two cervical vertebrae, the atlas and the axis, is called the atlanto-axial joint. This is a pivot joint and so allows rotational movement. This joint allows a 'no' type shake of the head.

Appreciating flexion at the poll

The articulation between the first and second cervical vertebrae is the same in people as it is in horses. Feeling the articulation in your own neck can be useful in understanding how your horse moves his head. Place your fingers on the vertebrae at the back of your neck. Nod and shake your head feeling where the majority of the movement comes from.

Flexion at the poll may be inhibited by:
• tension or spasm in the muscles of the poll
• the jaw being locked or clamped
• extension of the atlanto-occipital junction
• resistance
• psychological tension or nervousness.

Most of the rotational movement of the head comes from the atlanto-axial joint.

How tension in the poll affects movement

Tension in the brachiocephalic muscle at the poll and in upper neck, which extends down to the lower neck and shoulders, can cause a restriction in the movement of the forelimbs via the brachiocephalic muscle's point of insertion into the humerus.

The poll is an important area for muscle attachment as well as being the point of attachment for the nuchal ligament. Tension here from any cause or discomfort, leads to tightening of the top line muscles of the neck, namely the splenius muscle. This can affect the muscles further along the dorsal chain, causing hollowing of the back and ultimately affecting engagement of the hind leg.

Ideally, symmetrical muscular development on either side of the poll and in the muscles of the upper neck will allow even flexion at the poll. If the lateral movement in the atlanto-occipital junction is reduced for any reason, the atlanto-axial joint may work to compensate. As the joints work in different planes, this may result in the nose being tilted to the side.

TOP TIP

- Flexion is only achieved if the horse is ridden softly. Hard, rigid hands, or the use of restrictive training aids, will cause the muscles around the poll do tighten thus inhibiting movement and creating tension.

A locked jaw

The muscles of the jaw and poll are really important in the circle of muscles (see pages 43–44). They affect the suppleness of the poll at the atlas and influence how the horse responds to the bit. The sternomandibular muscle, which runs from the sternum to the lower jaw, needs to be relaxed for the horse to accept the bit and produce a balanced head carriage. Tension from locking the jaw against pressure, or tightening of the muscles at the top of the neck that control flexion at the poll, can also be transferred to the rest of the body.

When the jaw and poll are relaxed and the hands soft, the horse gently chews on the bit, which stimulates the salivary glands. A moist mouth is a good thing. A dry clamped mouth and locked jaw is unyielding, unresponsive and uncomfortable, creates tension, and inhibits flexion of the poll. It can be caused by hard rigid hands or the use of restrictive training aids. However, excessive saliva, as seen in the picture below, may be a result of the horse being unable to swallow, either because the mouth is clamped shut, because the bit is too large, or because the muscles around the throat are being restricted.

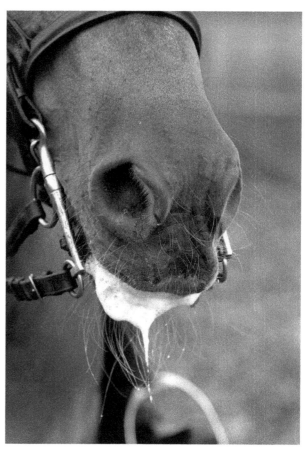

THE FUNCTION OF THE NUCHAL LIGAMENT

The nuchal ligament supports and holds the head and neck in position, allowing them to be raised and lowered. For its anatomy see page 23.

The head is the heaviest part of the body and together with the neck accounts for about one third of the horse's length. To hold the head and neck in a fixed position requires a great deal of muscular energy. The nuchal ligament is an energy-saving structure.

Lowering and lifting the head

When the horse is grazing or the head is down, the nuchal ligament, which attaches to the cervical vertebrae, is taught. This pulls on the supraspinous ligament, which attaches to the spinous processes of the thoracic vertebrae at the withers, prising them slightly apart. This in turn pulls on the spinous processes of the thoracic and lumbar vertebrae, causing the back to rise and the ribcage to lift.

When the head is raised, the nuchal ligament slackens and the neck hollows. The resulting lack of tension in the supraspinous ligament causes the back to hollow.

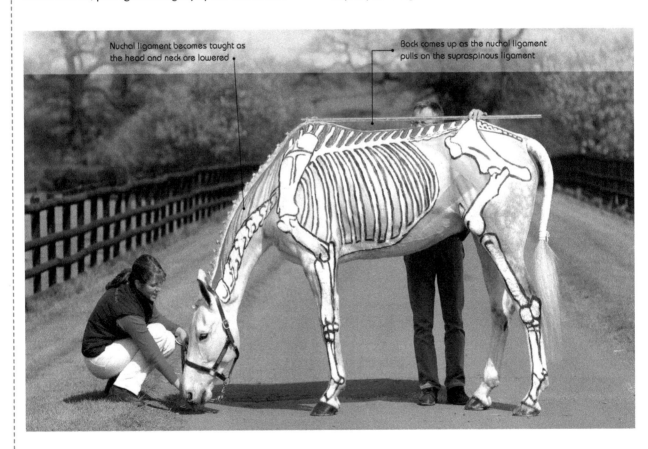

Nuchal ligament becomes taught as the head and neck are lowered

Back comes up as the nuchal ligament pulls on the supraspinous ligament

Nuchal ligament becomes slack as head and neck come up

Back lowers as there is no support through the supraspinous ligament

Associated muscles

The relationship between the position of the head and neck and the position of the back does not come from the nuchal ligament alone. The supraspinous, splenius, semispinalis and multifidus muscles with their diagonal directional 'pull' are part of the dorsal chain of top line muscles designed to lift the back. The 'pull' of these muscles on the back is increased when the head and neck are lowered, and so helps the horse support the weight of the rider.

Understanding the significance of the nuchal ligament in the context of the anatomy and physiology of the head and neck plays an important role in the training of the horse.

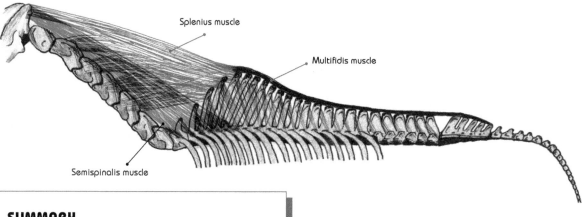

Splenius muscle

Multifidis muscle

Semispinalis muscle

SUMMARY
- The nuchal ligament supports the head and neck.
- When the head is down, the nuchal and supraspinous ligaments raise the back with no extra muscular effort.
- When the head is up, the neck hollows.

SPINAL POSTURE

Correct spinal posture is important for optimal performance and reducing the risk of back problems. To achieve this a horse should have well toned muscles, good confirmation, and correct head and neck carriage.

Spinal curves

The alignment of the horse's vertebrae creates a series of curves. The line of the curves follows the path of the vertebral bodies, above which are the vertebral arches that house the spinal cord. The natural configuration of the vertebrae is maintained by the strong ligaments and muscles supporting the back and by the abdominal muscles. In people, it is now well accepted that it is the core muscles that support the back. It is the same with the horse (see pages 82–83)

The natural curves of the spine are influenced by a number of factors. These include:
• the position of the head and neck. A high head carriage with a hollowed neck leads to a dipped back
• carrying the weight of the rider, which can invert the thoraco-lumbar curve particularly if the abdominal muscles are weak
• tight back or neck muscles anywhere within the dorsal chain. This can cause the horse to carry himself stiffly and also lead to misalignment of the axial skeleton
• conformational traits, such as sway back and ewe neck, both of which are undesirable
• loss of muscle tone through ageing.

Spinal posture

The position of the head and neck also has important implications for spinal posture. Ideally the thoraco-lumbar region of the spine should be straight or arched slightly upwards. Correct posture helps to maintain optimum performance of the spine, which, as it houses the central nervous system, plays an important role in coordination, movement, and maintaining balance as well as supporting the weight of the rider.

When the back curves downwards, it cannot work efficiently. This may put pressure on the spinal cord and the nerves that pass out between each vertebra. It also means that the dorsal spinal processes are pushed closer together

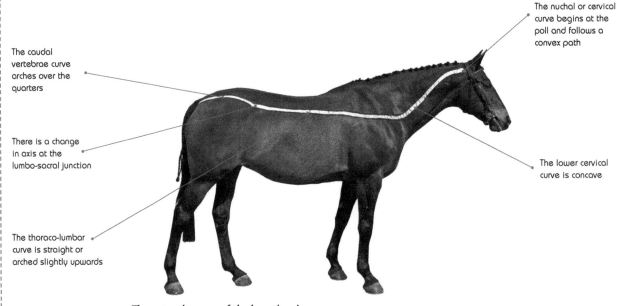

The caudal vertebrae curve arches over the quarters

There is a change in axis at the lumbo-sacral junction

The thoraco-lumbar curve is straight or arched slightly upwards

The nuchal or cervical curve begins at the poll and follows a convex path

The lower cervical curve is concave

The natural curves of the horse's spine.

and may even touch one another. Poor posture can be the cause of many muscular, ligamentary, and bony problems in the horse's back.

Optimal spinal posture can be achieved by correct training, recruitment of the core muscles, and by using correct positioning of the head and neck (see pages 77–78).

Concave curves in the back prevent the horse from carrying himself correctly. All ridden work will be adversely affected. If a horse raises his head and hollows his back, he cannot engage his hindquarters or step through effectively. It may also cause discomfort in the thoracic, lumbo-sacral and sacroiliac regions.

SUMMARY
- Correct positioning of the head and neck are important for good spinal posture.
- When the head is up and the nose forward, the back is down and the horse cannot engage behind.
- Correct spinal posture is important for optimal performance and reducing the risk of back problems.

HOW POSITIONING OF THE HEAD AND NECK AFFECTS THE WAY OF GOING

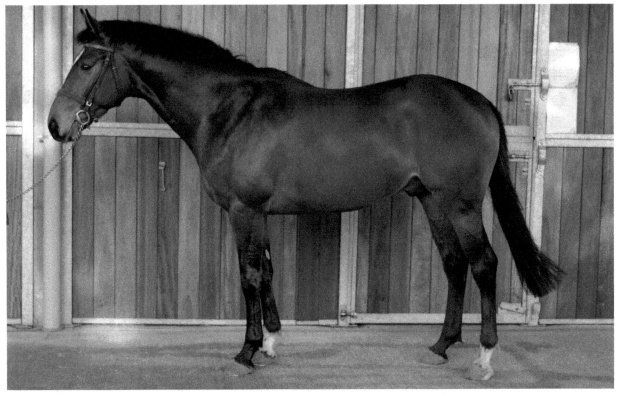

A long, arched, convex and relaxed neck is the result of correct riding.

To move efficiently and smoothly, the horse must be permitted to position his head and neck in a way that allows for free regular paces, balance and harmony. For the anatomy of the head and neck see pages 22–24.

Grazing position

In the field, horses spend approximately 60 per cent of their time grazing. The remainder is spent dozing or ambling with the head low. This is interspersed with occasional bursts of speed, perhaps shaking the head near the ground.

A small proportion of time is spent with the head raised, ears pricked, gazing into the distance. An even smaller proportion is spent in elevated movement with the head held high.

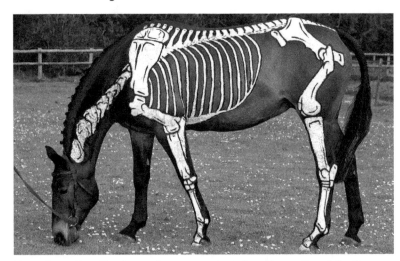

Here, the neck and back muscles are stretched along the topline whilst the abdominal muscles are contracted. The back and abdomen are raised due to the mechanics of the nuchal and supraspinous ligaments. This position is vital because it promotes correct posture.

Part two

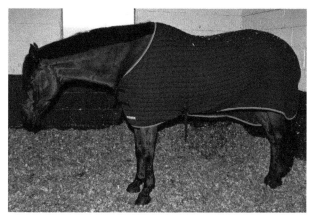

In the dozing position, the head and neck drop below wither height, the back is held in the correct anatomical posture and the stay apparatus is engaged.

Long and low neck position

Working the horse long and low mimics the grazing or dozing position allowing:
- the back to be raised through the mechanics of the nuchal and supraspinous ligaments
- correct alignment of the vertebrae
- the top line musculature to develop while maintaining suppleness and relaxation
- the spine to be flexed rather like a 'bow'. This contributes to supporting the weight of the rider (see pages 86–87)
- the longissimus dorsi muscle to be released allowing the back to swing and be suppled
- development of the abdominal muscles
- the protractor muscles to bring the hind leg well under
- unrestricted passage of spinal cord and nerves through the vertebral canal and intervertebral spaces.

As the horse progresses, working long and low:
- encourages the stride to become longer
- produces longitudinal suppleness as the back is raised and stretched
- encourages correct muscle recruitment
- promotes mental and physical relaxation
- develops proprioception and a sense of balance.

Long and low – an analgesic for horses!

- The spinous processes are pulled forward and upwards thus reducing the risk of kissing spines.
- The gaps between neighbouring vertebrae are maximized, allowing free passage of spinal nerves thus preventing pain, constriction, or irritation.
- Muscles are gently elongated.

Back problems can sometimes be alleviated by repositioning the head and neck during exercise!

TOP TIP

- Ride actively forward to enable the back to swing, the hind leg to step through, and to prevent running on to the forehand.

A more advanced horse working long and low.

Making the transition from long and low

Getting the head and neck into the correct position is a fundamental challenge for both horse and rider.

To progress to a **novice outline**, the poll must be raised to become the highest point while still keeping the frame long and the nose slightly in front of the vertical. Fundamentally this is a step towards self carriage, for which the horse requires:

• isometric contraction of the neck muscles
• well-conditioned back muscles supported by a strong core as dependency on the nuchal ligament decreases
• greater engagement to raise the back and allow more space for the hind limbs to come under
• the centre of gravity to move towards the rear as more of the weight is carried at the hind end
• the forehand to be lightened.

As this outline becomes established and the horse progresses, engagement will increase. The frame will become slightly more compressed, and the poll carried slightly higher as the horse matures both physically and mentally.

TOP TIPS

• Warm up for each training session working long and low to prepare the muscles.
• Work with impulsion, engagement, and straightness
• Sit up to lighten the forehand.
• Incorporate periods of stretching to relieve tension in muscles.
• Do not expect too much too soon. This outline can only be achieved gradually with patience and correct training.

How neck muscles develop with training

The aim of training the young horse is to develop slowly but surely the correct musculature to perform well in any discipline. This takes time and, after in hand work, can only be attained by riding long and low to achieve loose rhythmical and balanced paces. The neck muscles will only develop correctly if the horse is encouraged to work from behind. The head is initially supported by the nuchal ligament. Dependence on this diminishes as the muscles develop through isometric and eccentric muscle contraction. The young horse should not bring the head behind the vertical, nor should he run on into the hand.

TOP TIP

• It is muscularly tiring for a young horse to hold his neck isometrically in a fixed outline. Frequent rests are important. If he begins to fidget, stop what you are doing, and allow him to stretch down.

It is vital not to raise a young horse's head in training before his muscles are sufficiently developed.

Incorrect neck positions

The following head and neck positions are restrictive and detrimental to good movement.

Deep and round neck position – when taken to the extreme is also called hyperflexion. This neck position can cause train and hollowing in the lumbar section of the back. Movement is impeded by the centre of gravity being shifted forwards making the horse heavy on the forehand. This inhibits true collection by restricting the ability to step under, causing the hocks to trail.

Enormous tension is put on the nuchal and supraspinous ligaments, the upper neck, back muscles and fascia. Damage can be caused in the vertebrae and the airways may be restricted. This may be exacerbated by pain in the mouth, lower jaw and poll region

This unnatural posture in which the field of vision is restricted, can lead to a tension and stress with exaggerated, distorted or abnormal movement in the front legs at the expense of the natural flow, balance and confidence.

Over-bent neck position – riding the horse in this frame is not anatomically as extreme as hyperflexion, but is borne as a result of endeavouring to maintain an outline without focusing on working with engagement and impulsion. In a horse that is permanently over-bent, the affects on the horse both anatomically and with regard to performance are similar to hyper-flexion and can actually inhibit good movement.

'Broken' neck position – this is where the second or third cervical vertebrae, the weakest point in the horse's neck, is carried higher than the poll. This is the result of drawing the neck in from the hand rather than encouraging engagement from behind. Riding in this position will affect the ligaments of the back and the entire dorsal chain, thus creating an imbalance that inhibits engagement.

High and extended – overdeveloped muscles on the underside of the neck are indicative of incorrect training. The concave curve locks the neck, preventing lateral flexion and leading to a downward spiral of poor gaits, resistance, lack of concentration, incorrect muscle development, stress and tension.

SUMMARY

- The position of the head and neck has a direct influence on the horse's way of going.
- Working long and low, then progressively towards arched and elevated as the musculature allows, is the ideal and should be the aim of effective training.
- Restraining the position of the head and neck prevents correct recruitment of the back and abdominal muscles. It results in pain, discomfort, a hollowed back and restricted movement.
- Neck muscle development is a good indication of how well the horse uses his neck.

HOW THE HORSE SEES

The sense of sight is very important to the horse. He has almost all round vision and can scan his entire surroundings with only a slight movement of the head. Unlike us he has two types of vision and needs to position his head in order to focus.

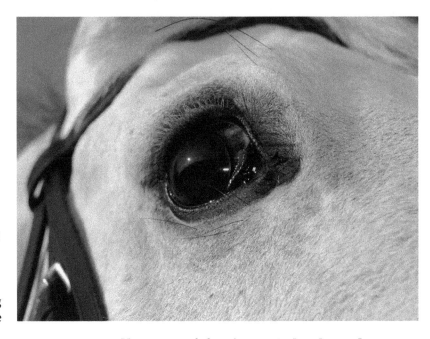

Monocular vision

Monocular vision allows the horse to see different things out of each eye. The horse's eyes are set wide apart and are large to enable him to detect the slightest motion. This allows for an increased field of vision enabling him to see from either side without turning his head. If a horse spooks, for example when a bird flies out from a hedge, it is because he has seen something with his monocular vision.

Binocular vision

Where the horse's field of vision overlaps, both eyes can focus on the same object. To judge distance, a horse uses its binocular vision. In this case, both eyes are directed down the nose. This means to look at an object in the distance the horse must raise his head. To look at an object on the ground, he must lower his head.

When he is grazing, the horse's gaze is directed at the ground in front of him but he will be using his monocular vision to be conscious of his surroundings. Should something attract his attention he will raise and turn his head to bring the binocular vision into effect.

How positioning of the head and neck affect sight

A horse approaching a jump needs to lift his head in order to assess the height and depth of the object with his binocular vision. It is important, therefore, to allow him to do this and for him not be hampered by too tight a martingale.

When a horse is flexed at the poll or being ridden 'on the bit' his field of vision, which is being directed towards the ground, is actually considerably restricted. There is a blind spot in front of the horse just about the width of his body. This illustrates how much trust a horse needs to have in the rider. If the horse is being ridden in hyperflexion, this is even more the case as the field of vision is being directed backwards along the nose towards the feet and the horse is literally being ridden 'blind'.

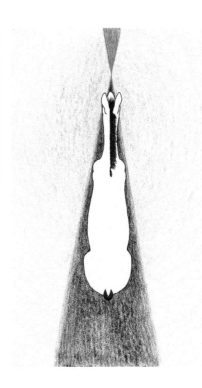

Blind Spots

- The horse has a blind spot directly behind him. This is why we should always approach the horse from the side.
- The horse has a blind spot directly in front of his forehead.
- The horse cannot focus on an object less than one and a half metres (five feet) in front of him.
- If you can't see either of the horse's eyes, he can't see you!

Why horses are 'jumpy' in the wind

The horse's large eyes are able to detect moving objects easily. On a windy day, there are just too many moving objects, which makes him uneasy. When a horse spooks, having seen something fluttering to the side, he will run first and investigate later! This is why in the field, if a horse is alarmed, he will run, then stop, turn around, lift his head and gaze at it.

Light sensitivity

Research has shown that horses do have some night vision. Because their eyes are sensitive to weak light, they can see fairly well at dusk and dawn, but they lack the ability to adjust their eyes to darkness very quickly. This is why they exhibit sometimes reluctance to enter a dark building or a horse box from bright sunshine.

Some horses find it tricky to jump from sunshine to shade.

SUMMARY
- **Horses have both monocular and binocular vision.**
- **When working on the bit, their vision is restricted.**
- **Horses need to position their heads appropriately in order to focus on an object in front of them.**

Seeing colour

Human eyes have three types of light sensitive cells. This means we can see all colours. Horses only have two types, which means they see fewer colours.

CORE STABILITY

Core stability refers to the well toned muscle systems that help to maintain good posture and give a solid foundation for movement and balance. It enables a horse to recruit the musculature of the trunk effectively and thus influence the position and stability of the spine and pelvis during dynamic movements. This is particularly significant in maintaining self carriage, carrying the weight of the rider, performing highly engaged dressage movements, and jumping and working at speed.

The benefits of a strong core

In humans, a strong core acts like a corset, encircling the trunk and strengthening and protecting the back.
In the horse strong core muscles result in:
• good balance and overall muscular strength
• good spinal posture
• security through the spine, hips and pelvis
• enhanced performance
• ease of movement
• reduced risk of injury
• improved self-carriage
• the ability to maintain self-carriage and a correct way of going for a longer periods
• smooth, efficient, well coordinated movement.

Conversely, weak core stability can lead to fatigue, loss of balance and control, poor performance and increased risk of injury particularly in the region of the back, neck and pelvis. For ways to strengthen the core, see pages 125–133.

The muscles involved in core stability

The muscles involved in core stability are generally smaller and deeper responsible for posture and stability, rather than the large, gymnastic, superficial muscles.

The back muscles – the deep back muscles, for example the multifidus, tend to be smaller, interweaving and connecting one or two vertebrae in a long continuous chain, stabilizing them and maintaining correct posture. They are well developed in horses with good core strength.

The abdominal muscles – these are principally the internal and external abdominal oblique muscles, the rectus abdominae and the transverse abdominal muscle. As well as supporting the viscera, they also stabilize, lift and flex the back by increasing the intra-abdominal pressure.
They lift the back during the suspension phase of the stride. The rectus abdominae has extra layers of muscle supported by strong sheets of connective tissue. These muscles, as part of the ventral chain, help support the core. Horses with toned, well conditioned abdominals, often appear slimmer. Weak abdominals sag – the equivalent of a beer belly!

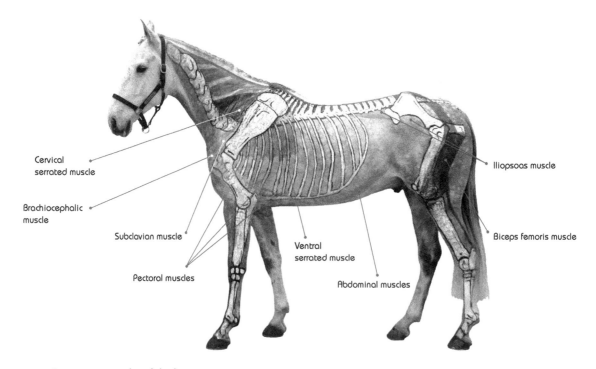

Cervical serrated muscle

Brachiocephalic muscle

Subclavian muscle

Pectoral muscles

Ventral serrated muscle

Abdominal muscles

Iliopsoas muscle

Biceps femoris muscle

Some core muscles of the horse.

Iliopsoas muscles – these sub-lumbar muscles are involved in stabilizing the pelvis by supporting and flexing the lumbo-sacral junction and sacroiliac area.

The iliopsoas muscle group helps to tilt the pelvis, stabilize the spine in the lumbar region, and shift the centre of gravity backwards. They run from the under side of the lumbar vertebrae to under and inside the pelvis and hip joint. They are important in collection, enabling the pelvis to tuck under and the hind legs to step through.

These muscles are so deep that they cannot be felt or influenced through massage or physical therapy.

The hip stabilizers – as well as deeper muscles the biceps femoris is one of the main muscles involved in stabilizing the hip. It is important in turning at speed, and in advanced movements, such as the canter pirouette, where only one hind limb is on the ground. Pelvic and hip stability reduces the risk of strain in the lumbar region.

The thoracic sling – this includes the serratus muscle, which fans out from the underside of the scapula to the last four cervical vertebrae and the first eight ribs, and the pectoral muscles, which attach from the inside of the scapula and humerus on to the sternum, connecting the forelegs to the lower part of the ribcage and lifting the withers between the shoulder blades. The thoracic sling is reinforced by the latissimus dorsi muscle and contributes to a strong core.

Even when the horse has finished growing, as the thoracic sling muscles become stronger and more conditioned with work, they will shorten, lift the thorax up between the forelimbs, and give the illusion of the horse growing in height.

SUMMARY
- **Core stability provides the strength and coordination of muscles during movement.**
- **Strengthening the core stabilizing muscles can reduce injuries and enhance athletic performance.**
- **Core strength in the horse comes from well developed deep vertebral, abdominal and illiopsoas muscles, hip stabilizers and thoracic sling muscles.**

In order to maintain pelvic stability, the hind, abdominal and back muscles have to work together.

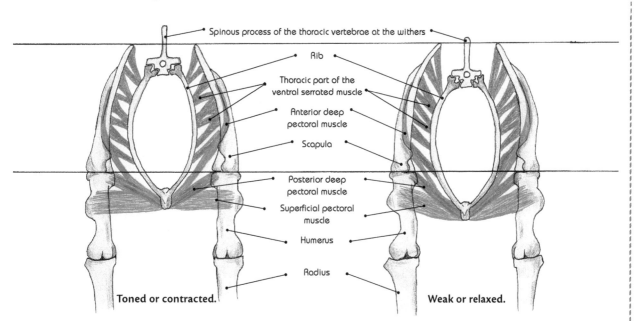

Spinous process of the thoracic vertebrae at the withers

Rib

Thoracic part of the ventral serrated muscle

Anterior deep pectoral muscle

Scapula

Posterior deep pectoral muscle

Superficial pectoral muscle

Humerus

Radius

Toned or contracted.

Weak or relaxed.

When the thoracic sling muscles contract they lift the withers up in between the shoulder blades.

The way of going

IMPULSION

Impulsion is pushing power. It is the thrust produced when energy created in the hind limb is converted to forward movement. A horse is working with impulsion when it pushes off to move powerfully and energetically forward. This is not speed alone. The Germans use the term 'swung', which means moving with a spring in the step. The greater the impulsion, the longer the moment of suspension. A horse can only have impulsion if his hind legs are engaged and his back supple, allowing the power to come through from behind.

The muscles a horse uses for kicking are the same as those he uses for propulsion.

Hocks under.

Why we need it

Impulsion maximizes natural athletic ability by making the paces elastic, light, and expressive. This provides the power required to perform, particularly those movements requiring high levels of collection.

Impulsion is as important in jumping as it is in dressage because it is the contained power that allows the horse to propel himself successfully over an obstacle.

Hocks trailing.

How to create impulsion

Good attitude is an essential ingredient for impulsion. The horse must be fit, energetic and keen. A slow, sluggish, bored horse will not move with impulsion. To create it:

• the horse must step through from behind really bringing his hind legs underneath his body. This is often called 'hocks under' and involves recruiting the protractor chain of muscles down the front of the hind limb to bring the leg forward. The further the horse engages his hind leg, the more impulsion can be created

• as the horse bears weight on the hind limb, the hip, stifle, and hock joint by virtue of the reciprocal system, flexes in the stance phase. This can sometimes give the appearance of 'sitting behind'. It is hard work for the muscles of the hind legs, which support the joints and leg with isometric and eccentric muscle contraction

Flexion of the joints in the hindquarters is seen best in the support phase of the stride in a movement of a slower tempo. The decrease in joint angles allows the horse to push off the ground with greater dynamics, impulsion and spring.

- the muscles down the back of the leg particularly the hamstrings, and gluteals, contract concentrically to propel the body forward over the foot
- the head and neck need to be telescoped out forwards in order to achieve maximum extension of the hip joint and therefore maximum thrust. This is why to be able lengthen the stride in extended paces the frame must also be lengthened

- the pushing force must travel through a relaxed, elastic, swinging back in order to achieve true impulsion. As the hind leg pushes and the gluteals contract, the longissimus dorsi muscle will also contract both to control and direct the energy and to support the spine. The horse must be straight so that the energy can be transferred efficiently forwards through the spine.

TOP TIPS

- Keep schooling sessions a sensible length. Little and often is more productive.
- Make sure the horse is in front of your leg.
- Hill work, jumping and canter work help to build the extensor muscles of the hind leg, which are important for impulsion.

Notice how in both of these pictures the horses have extended their head and neck out forwards in order to achieve maximal extension of the hip joint.

Foster *joie de vivre*! Engage in agility and strengthening activities that the horse will enjoy – hacking, hill work, jumping, cross-country, fun rides and team chasing.

The way of going

HOW THE HORSE CARRIES THE WEIGHT OF THE RIDER

The two most important functions of the horse's back are to transmit propulsive forces forwards and to support weight. The strength of the back comes from the configuration of the vertebrae and the spinal ligaments, tendons, and muscles that ensure the spine remains relatively rigid. The correct posture of the horse's back, throughout the thoraco-lumbar section, is for the vertebral bodies to form a slightly convex arc or 'bow', which is tensioned by the ventral chain of muscles (see pages 43–44).

Strong back

It is the spine together with its supporting ligaments, particularly the ventral longitudinal ligament, which supports the weight of the rider. The deep muscles in the back also play an important role as without this supporting musculature the horse's back would not maintain good posture. A horse can reasonably carry up to about 25 per cent of its body weight.

Importance of abdominal and core muscles

In order to carry the weight of the rider, it is imperative that the horse has strong abdominal muscles. These form part of the ventral muscle chain, which lift and support the back and maintain the pelvic tilt. Without a strong core, the horse cannot properly use his back or hindquarters. Weak abdominal muscles cause the natural curvature of the spine to sag. This can be accompanied by a large hanging abdomen.

It is the recruitment of the abdominal muscles that helps to support and lift the back, this is why it is often said that with no abdominals there is no back!

The thoracic sling muscles, in particular the pectoral and serrated muscles are also recruited in supporting the weight of the rider. However, this can only happen if the horse is engaging his abdominal muscles and stepping through from behind.

The position of the head and neck

Lowering of the horse's head and neck causes the back to raise and strengthen. This is why it can be beneficial to work our horses long and low (see page 77). The dorsal muscle chain in conjunction with the nuchal and supraspinous ligaments, supported by the core strength of the abdominal muscles, allows the horse to carry weight. A high head carriage causes the back to dip and loose some of its strength.

Engagement of the hind limbs

The muscles that allow the horse to bring his hind legs underneath him are part of the ventral chain. The further the hind legs come under the body, the more the back has to lift to allow the engagement. Also, the harder the abdominal muscles have to work, the stronger the back becomes.

The hindquarters can only truly engage if the forehand and back are lifted. Conversely, the forehand and back can only be lifted, supporting the weight of the rider, if the hindquarters are engaged.

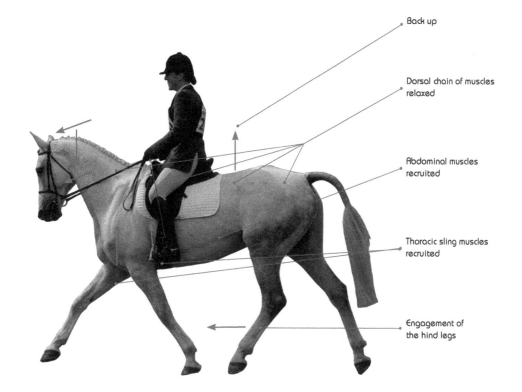

Back up

Dorsal chain of muscles relaxed

Abdominal muscles recruited

Thoracic sling muscles recruited

Engagement of the hind legs

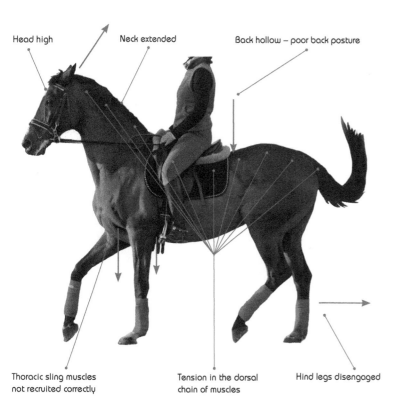

Head high

Neck extended

Back hollow – poor back posture

Thoracic sling muscles not recruited correctly

Tension in the dorsal chain of muscles

Hind legs disengaged

SUMMARY

- Although there are many contributory factors, the spine and ligaments provide the main support in carrying the weight of the rider.
- The ventral chain of muscles, provide the main muscular support for the vertebral column.
- The stronger the core muscles, the greater the ability to maintain correct posture and the greater the weight bearing capacity.
- Engagement of the hind limb supports the back as does lowering the head and neck.

The way of going

MAINTAINING STRAIGHTNESS

Straightness is a desirable quality. It makes for ease of training, allows us to 'ride up the centre line' without wavering, and approach a jump without deviating.

A horse can be considered straight when his forehand is in line with his hindquarters or when his longitudinal axis is in line with the straight or curved track it is following. Straightness is a result of good conformation, symmetrical muscle development, good training and a perfectly balanced rider. If the horse is straight, the hind legs will push exactly in the direction of the centre of gravity.

What causes crookedness?

Animals are often asymmetrical and most horses are crooked in some way. This this may be caused by a number of factors.

Rider crookedness – an asymmetrical rider will cause a horse to become asymmetrical because of having to continually compensate for carrying an unequal load, and coping with unequal aids.

Riders are often the root of this problem.

Structural imbalance – this can be congenital. For example, one leg of a horse may be shorter than the other.

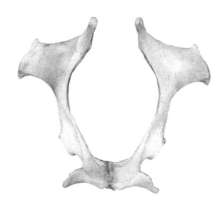

Look closely! This pony's pelvis demonstrates asymmetry.

Right or left sided dominance – this has its origins in the brain hemispheres. Evidence of forelimb dominance can sometimes be seen when striking off in canter, taking off or landing from a jump, or pawing the floor in the stable. Horses are naturally stiffer on one rein than the other, resulting in the quarters swinging out or having difficulty bending through the neck and body.

Conditioning – unequal work loads, for example, working more on one rein than the other or always leading and mounting from the same side, can lead to unequal muscle development.

Horses often learn from an early age that pressure on the nose means 'turn head to the left'.

Discomfort or pain – this can result from any of the horse's body systems not just the musculo-skeletal system. Discomfort can be the cause of crookedness and is sometimes evident, for example, when a mare is in season.

Previous injury – accidents that result in soft or hard tissue injury can make a horse asymmetrical, particularly if there is muscle wastage.

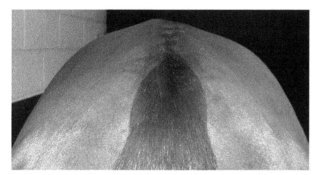

Unequal heights of the tuber sacrale, when the horse is standing square, may be attributable to a previous fracture of the iliac wing of the pelvis.

Anatomical implications of crookedness

If a horse cannot move in a straight line, there may be anatomical reasons for this.

Back compensations – when the hind limbs push the body forwards, they transmit energy through the sacroiliac joint and into the spine. The back muscles contract to support the joints of the vertebrae and to help maintain vertebral straightness. If one hind leg continually pushes harder than the other, this may result in crooked movement.

Compensation for these unequal forces transmitted to the back is provided by:
• the multifidus, the small postural muscles interweaving between the vertebrae which are the main stabilizers that keep the spine straight
• slight rotational movements within the lumbar vertebrae
• the large superficial muscles of the back that work to maintain the direction of movement, for example, the longissimus dorsi.

Asymmetrical muscle development – this is a chicken and egg situation! Unequal muscle development can be either a symptom or a cause of crooked movement. It can result from previously torn muscle, scar tissue, pain, discomfort, unbalanced training and conditioning, or one-sided dominance. In the latter case, as the dominant side becomes strengthened, increased usage will lead to greater muscle development on that side.

In severe cases, continually moving with a crooked posture may lead to curvature of the spine. The resultant stresses on the vertebrae can also upset the normal balance of the central nervous system.

Assessing crookedness

Use mirrors to assess your riding position to ensure you are sitting centrally with weight evenly distributed – head straight, shoulders level, hands even, and stirrups the same length. Check if the horse is twisting his nose to one side, or if he is moving on two or three tracks. Look to see if he is leaning in or out and whether his quarters swing to the inside or the outside.

From the ground, watch as he moves away and towards you. Does he track up evenly? Is his muscular development noticeably different on one side than the other?

What to do

If you are concerned about crookedness, it may be worth seeing a therapist to work on your own body, and enlisting the help of a trainer or equine therapist to assist with your horse.

A good way to assess your horse's symmetry is to stand on a block behind him. Ensure that he is standing square, and is looking straight ahead.

TOP TIPS

• Ensure you are sitting straight. A crooked rider cannot make a straight horse.
• School equally on both reins to develop balanced strength and suppleness.
• Working on circles and serpentines helps improve bending and flexibility on the stiffer side.

THE GAITS

Knowledge, recognition and understanding of how the horse executes each pace correctly will enable the rider to assess movement, improve the quality of the gaits, understand what he is feeling, and perform ridden exercises correctly.

This chapter covers:

• walk

• trot

• canter

• gallop

WALK

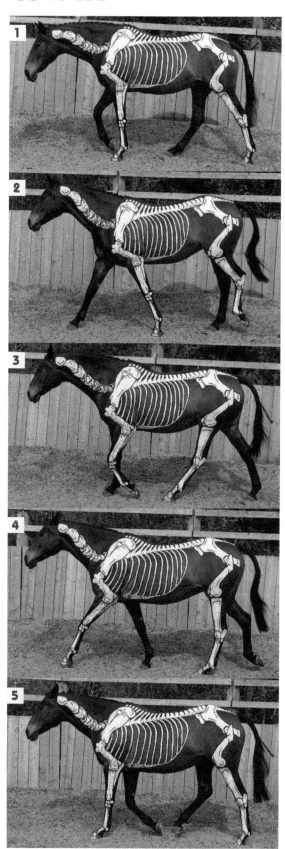

The walk.

The walk is a four-beat gait, averaging four miles per hour. One foot is always raised as the other three are on the ground, except for a brief moment when weight is being transferred from one foot to another. Ideally, the advancing rear hoof oversteps the spot where the previously placed front hoof made ground contact. The head and neck move slightly up and down to help maintain balance.

The footfalls

The sequence that your horse's hooves touch the ground in walk is:
• Right Hind (RH) : Right Fore (RF) :
  Left Hind (LH) : Left Fore (LF)

The four beat time should be evenly paced:
1-2-3-4 – 1-2-3-4

Irregularities in the sound may be a result of lameness or due to the forelimbs and hind limbs *of the same side* moving almost on the same beat. This is known as a lateral walk and then the beat will sound slightly irregular:
1-2–3-4 – 1-2–3-4.

Types and qualities of walk

A good walk displays even, active, rhythmical steps with impulsion. This is achieved through supple muscles, a swinging back and flexible joints. Energy is the final ingredient needed for a good walk. Within dressage there are four types of walk that are recognized.

Medium walk – this is an energetic, regular walk with steps of moderate length and the horse working on the bit, maintaining a light steady contact. The hind limbs overtrack.

Collected walk – this has higher, shorter steps; the hindquarters are engaged, the head and neck is arched and raised with the horse in self carriage.

Extended walk – here the horse covers as much ground as possible while remaining on the bit without losing the regularity of the steps. The entire frame is elongated.

Free walk – the horse is allowed complete freedom to lower and stretch out his head and neck. He must overtrack whilst maintaining the regular four beats.

TOP TIP

• A good walk, particularly with a young horse, is the most difficult pace to achieve and the easiest to destroy. Begin by aiming for a good medium or free walk, gradually asking the horse to come on the bit.

TROT

The trot is a two beat symmetrical gait. The working trot averages five to eight miles per hour. This is a stable gait where the horse moves his legs in diagonal pairs separated by a moment of suspension. The head and neck are kept still as balancing adjustments are unnecessary.

The footfalls

The sequence in which the horse's hooves touch the ground in trot is:
• RH and LF : Suspension : LH and RF : Suspension

The two time beat should be evenly spaced. 1-2 – 1-2. An uneven beat denotes lameness.

Types and qualities of trot

Steps should be light, balanced, steady, regular and rhythmical, with knees and hocks flexing to the same height. The head should be steady and the forelimbs and hind limbs equally active. A supple back should allow the horse to overtrack as he steps through evenly. This is essential for extended paces.

There are four basic types of trot, although there are other variations. The basic types of trot are demarked mainly by change in stride length with only small adjustments in rate.

Working trot – this is the most natural trot. The horse should be on the bit, nose vertical or slightly in front of the vertical, swinging through with active, rhythmical, balanced steps, tracking up or overtracking with good hock action and impulsion derived from the hindquarters.

Collected trot – this is a very engaged trot with the frame compressed and most weight carried by the hindquarters. Steps are shorter, higher and more energetic than in working trot. The neck is raised and arched with increased lightness and mobility of the shoulders. The hocks should be well engaged, and the horse should remain on the bit.

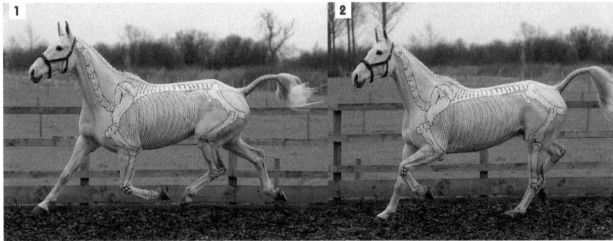

Medium trot – between working and extended trot and with impulsion coming from the hindquarters, this balanced pace, with moderately lengthened strides, is performed on the bit with the nose slightly in front of the vertical and the neck slightly extended and lowered. Steps should be even and rhythmical with the frame longer than the working trot, but rounder than the extended trot.

Extended trot – performed on the bit, with round back, head in front of the vertical, more weight on the hindquarters and a stretched frame. This is a balanced, rhythmical elegant, engaged trot with long elevated strides and maximum suspension.

The contribution of the hind limb

As with all paces, most of the power comes from the hind limbs. In trot, extra propulsion is derived from the toe digging into the ground at the point of maximum protraction, pivoting slightly, then pushing the body forwards.

The contribution of the forelimb

Although the main function of the forelimb is balance and control, in some instances of trot, trotting uphill for example, and in horses with a well developed brachiocephalic muscle, it can slightly pull the horse forwards. This muscle, which runs from the back of the skull and cervical vertebrae one to four down to humerus in the foreleg, also affects the positioning of the head and neck, causing the head to swing from side to side as the muscles become tired.

TOP TIPS

- Establish a good even working trot before asking the horse for either lengthened steps or collection.
- Try to ensure the horse does not run on the forehand by sitting up and controlling the speed with your rising.
- Ensure that this gait is well established before making the transition from rising to sitting trot.

The footfalls of trot:
(1) suspension (1)...
(2 and 3) LH and RF...
(4) suspension...
(5 and 6) RH and LF...
(7) suspension.

CANTER

The canter is a controlled asymmetrical, three-beat jumping gait. It is basically a variation of a slow gallop. The speed within the gait varies considerably up to about 17 miles per hour. Momentum carries the horse forward and helps to maintain balance, even when there is only one leg on the ground.

The footfalls

The sequence in which the hooves touch the ground in canter is:
• left lead – RH : LH and RF : LF : suspension
• right lead – LH : RH and LF : RF : suspension

The three-time beat should be evenly spaced and separated by a moment of suspension. 1-2-3 – 1-2-3. The faster the horse moves, the longer the moment of suspension.

In collection with little impulsion, a fourth beat may be heard as the limbs synchronize as in a slow gallop (see pages 96–97). This is termed a four-beat canter and is recognized as incorrect movement.

The canter.

Types and qualities of canter

Striking off with the outside hind and leading with the inside fore, a good canter should demonstrate regularity, engagement, impulsion, rhythm, balance and straightness.

Although there are variations, there are four main types of canter achieved by altering the stride length while keeping the stride rate relatively constant.

Working canter – this is the most natural canter. The horse should go forwards on the bit with light, regular, balanced strides, good hock action, impulsion and a discernible period of suspension.

Collected canter – shorter and springier than working canter, this is performed on the bit with the neck raised and

arched, the frame more compressed and more weight on the quarters. It displays lightness, mobility of the shoulders, more engagement and suppleness through the back.

Medium canter – this balanced rounded canter, between working and extended, is performed on the bit with the neck slightly lowered and the nose in front of the vertical. Strides should be long, even and energetic.

Extended canter – remaining rhythmical, in this canter the frame lengthens as the head and neck are lowered with the nose pointing forward. Stride length and impulsion increase to the maximum, covering as much ground as possible.

TOP TIPS

- Establish a good even rhythm in the working canter before asking for collection or extension.
- Allow your hands to follow the action of the head and neck, particularly in the bigger canters as this will assist the mechanics and balance of the movement.

Counter-canter – this is a movement where the horse leads on a circle with the outside fore. This exercise requires suppleness through the shoulder and back. Natural flexion is maintained with the poll to the outside. This is often used as an exercise to straighten the horse.

How the horse uses his body in canter

- As the hind legs come through almost simultaneously, the front end is raised, the back is lifted and rounded and the pelvis tucked under.
- As the hind legs thrust backward propelling the horse forwards, the neck extends forward and then down as the leading forelimb touches the ground. More weight is taken on the forelimb.
- As the forelimbs thrust, momentum carries the body forward and over the front limbs.
- The forelimbs push the front end upwards creating the moment of suspension. This upward thrust also helps push the weight rearwards allowing the head and neck to come up and back and bringing the hind limbs under the body. This produces a rocking motion.

GALLOP

The gallop.

Covering more ground than the canter, the gallop is a naturally extended asymmetrical, four-beat gait with dynamic balance and low, free moving head carriage. It can reach speeds of up to 55mph. There are never more than two feet on the ground and usually only one. When all four feet are off the ground, they are bent rather than extended. As in canter the horse strikes off with the non-leading hind foot.

The footfalls

The sequence in which the hooves touch the ground is as follows:
• **left lead** – RH : LH : RF : LF : suspension
• **right lead** – LH : RH : LF : RF : suspension

The gallop is a four-time beat separated by a moment of suspension, which is sometimes difficult to discern. It is often described as thundering.

The walk is a good indicator as to the quality of the gallop, especially with regards to length of stride. This is why it is interesting to watch horses walk around the paddock before they race.

Racing gallop

A racehorse can gallop at approximately 40–45mph over about 1 mile. Quarter horses can reach up to 55mph in sprint races over the shorter distance. A racehorse's stride length at gallop is 7–8 metres (23–26 foot) long. At maximum speed, a racehorse can achieve up to 3 strides per second. A breath is taken during each moment of suspension, resulting of a respiration rate of up to 180 breaths per minute.

Contribution of the body and limbs

Head and neck – by carrying the head and neck lower and telescoped out whilst galloping, the horse can alter his centre of gravity, fully extend his hip, improve balance, increase momentum, maximize stride length and help propel himself forwards.

Forelimbs – in gallop the forelimbs contribute as much to propulsion as the hind limbs. As he gathers momentum, his toe digs in to the ground helping to propel him forwards and up into the moment of suspension.

Sacroiliac area, abdomen and back – during the swing phase, just as the hind feet touch the ground, the horse uses his abdominal muscles to lift

his back. Along with the sacroiliac joint, the increase in thoraco-lumbar flexion enables the lumbo-sacral junction to flex efficiently, bringing the hind legs further under the body. Flexion in the lumbo-sacral junction ensures maximum transfer of energy forwards, enables the legs to come through together and the stride length to increase.

Hind limbs – the more powerfully the hind feet strike the ground and the shorter the period of time between the footfalls, the more effective the forward propulsion and the greater the speed. To achieve maximum thrust when coming out of a starting gate or when jumping, the horse uses both hind limbs simultaneously.

Skeleton and ligaments – the faster the gallop, the greater the ground reaction forces. This causes the suspensory ligament to reach full stretch, causing the fetlock to touch the ground.

Towards the end of a race, it is possible for a horse's muscles to become so tired that the support work is taken over by the skeleton and ligaments.

TOP TIPS

- Before galloping, horses should be warmed up for at least twenty minutes to ensure the muscle and respiratory systems are ready for action and to reduce the risk of tendon and ligament damage.
- Pull up slowly through the paces after galloping to allow the muscles to adjust.
- Horses should be walked for twenty minutes after galloping to allow the safe removal of toxins from the blood and to return heart and respiration rates to normal.

The fetlock circled is in hyperextension and is touching the ground.

HOW THE HORSE JUMPS – AN ANATOMICAL APPROACH

The ability of the horse to jump is determined by conformation, anatomy, gymnastic ability, technique and training. Although the horse is a very good athlete, he is not a natural jumper. This is due to his large head, heavy gut, and the relative rigidity of his spine.

Successful jumping is dependant on the horse's ability to create enough force during take off for all parts of his body to clear the object in a perfect parabola (see page 104), the highest point of which is over the highest point of the jump. His musculature must be sufficiently developed and conditioned to allow him to do this. The quarters need to be strong and powerful and the scapula should slope well back to allow the shoulder to rise and the front legs to tuck up.

Jumping involves a series of complex movement and reflex patterns, which require rhythm, tempo, impulsion and balance. These can take a long time to become established. Sound training and regular practice will ensure that the learned responses become automatic, rather like us driving a car.

This chapter covers the five phases to the jump:

• approach

• take off

• suspension

• landing

• recovery

How the horse jumps

APPROACH

The approach is the planning and preparation phase. Good planning provides the best opportunity for a successful jump. A horse that weaves its way towards an obstacle, backing off or grinding to a near halt will not make a good jump.

As the horse first sees the obstacle and appraises the effort required, he will often raise his head and neck, using his binocular vision to focus or 'lock on' to the fence. It is important that he should be allowed to do this.

Prerequisites for a good approach

In order to make a good jump, it is important to approach the obstacle correctly.

- A balanced, good quality, regular three beat canter is essential. The horse should be collected, engaged, going forward with impulsion and be able to lengthen and shorten the stride without altering the speed or rhythm of the gait. A good collected canter allows him to gather his energy, round his back and get his hindquarters well under ready to propel himself into the air. The bigger the fence, the better the quality of canter required.
- The approach must be straight in order to allow the horse to see where he is going and to give him time to judge the height and distance of the fence. This also assists his balance.
- The rider must sit up on the approach in order to minimize the load on the forehand and to allow the horse to come up through the shoulder on take off.

What happens as the horse approaches the jump

Three strides before the fence a horse makes the following adjustments:

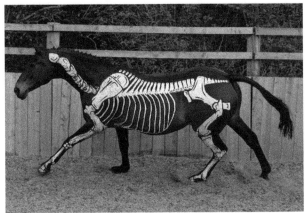

- on the third to last stride before take-off the horse will lengthen his frame

- on the penultimate stride, the head and neck is brought forward and down. This lowers the horse's centre of gravity as he prepares to launch himself upwards. Human high jumpers also use this technique

Not all horses jump in the same way. Head and neck positions will vary on the approach, as will limb positions over the jump. Some horses 'snap' their front legs up more than others. The horse uses the positioning of his head and neck on the approach to either draw into or back off the fence.

TOP TIPS

- Practise lengthening and shortening the canter stride whilst keeping a balanced and rhythmical canter. Place two poles approximately 20 paces apart. Increase and decrease the number of strides between them.
- Jump as many small and varied obstacles as possible to ensure that the horse can jump out of his stride and approach any type of jump with confidence.

- on the last stride the canter will dissociate as the diagonal pair of limbs come down separately resulting in a four-beat stride. The horse will lift his head and neck to lighten the forehand in preparation for take off. This stride is shorter and quicker as the horse gathers himself ready to spring.

At this point it is essential for the rider both to sit up, in order to avoid loading extra weight on to the forehand and to bring the hands forward to allow the head and neck to telescope out.

A bad jump is often a result of a poor approach and will destroy a horse's confidence both in himself and the rider. Confidence can be destroyed in seconds but takes hours to rebuild. In order to avoid pitfalls it is worth practising the 'five p' principle with regard to the approach – proper planning prevents poor performance.

Encourage the horse to approach the jump straight by using strategically placed poles.

TAKE OFF

The take off is the most important phase of jumping as the thrust determines the height, width, distance and speed of the leap. Once airborne, these cannot be altered.

Prerequisites for a good take off

- A good balanced approach, combined with straightness and confidence, is crucial for a good take off. A horse that arrives unbalanced and anxious at the wrong point will not make a good jump.
- The rider must incline the upper body forward, remain in balance and ensure the hands allow enough rein for the head to extend. This gives the horse the best possible opportunity to make a good jump.

What happens at take off

On the last stride before making a jump the horse prepares to launch – the head and neck will come up quickly to shift the centre of gravity backwards thus lightening the fore hand in preparation for the forelimbs to thrust.

Young or inexperienced horses tend to take a really good look at a fence as they approach. This means that often they do not raise their head and neck until the very last moment at take off.

- Take off is initiated by the forelimbs, which push the front end up.
- The trailing forelimb propels the horse upwards. This takes approximately one and half times the horse's body weight. The forces in the leading forelimb are less. On take off, the fetlock extends via the superficial and deep digital flexor tendons and parent muscles and in some cases the joint will touch the ground. Like people, horses can be stronger on one side than the other and may have a preferred take off leg. This explains why some horses change legs just before a jump.

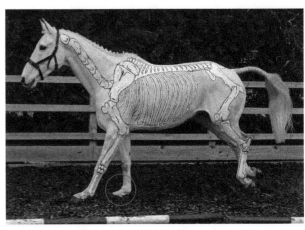

As the forelimbs stretch out, a slight braking force converts forward movement to upward momentum. The trailing fetlock demonstrates a greater degree of extension through the joint than the leading one.

- The front end is pushed into the air by the triceps brachii, biceps brachii and supraspinatus muscles straightening the joints of the shoulder and elbow. At the same time the thoracic sling muscles contract to lift the thorax between the scapulae. The centre of gravity moves back as the body rises between the scapulae to meet the raised head and neck, which are then lowered as the contraction of the brachiocephalic muscles brings the forelimbs forwards and up.
- As the forelimbs leave the ground, pushing the front end up, they are very quickly replaced by the hind limbs coming through virtually in unison.

The moment of suspension in the take off stride is very short.

- The power required for take off is created by the muscles of the protractor chain, which brings the hind legs further under the body, and the length of the stance phase, which is slightly longer in relation to a normal canter stride. Flexion at the lumbo-sacral junction and hip is also increased. This gives the appearance of the pelvis tilting and tucking under.

The hamstring muscle group contracts to extend the hip joint and initiate the upward thrust by driving the feet against the ground.

• The final push comes from the straightening of the fetlock via the action of the digital flexor muscles.

As the hind feet prepare to leave the ground, the head and neck are telescoped forwards. This allows maximum extension of the hip joint and to helps direct the thrust.

• At the actual moment of take off the hind limbs will be extended and the forelimbs will flex. The head and neck are extended forwards and down. The take off phase ends as the hind feet leave the ground.

TOP TIPS

• Practise aiming at a given spot consistently by lengthening and shortening the stride.
• Practise riding to a fence in a consistent rhythm, resisting altering the speed immediately before the jump.
• Avoid overloading the horse's forehand by leaning too far forward.

The gluteals are then activated to push the body forwards and upwards. At this point that they work with the longissimus dorsi muscles to raise the forehand still further.

The perfect take off spot

The height and the width of the jump are determined at take off. Arriving at the perfect take off spot can sometimes seem a challenge. As jumping is an upward projection of a normal canter stride, being able to adjust the stride length a few strides out from the jump without altering the speed or tempo is an advantage.

Good technique

When assessing good jumping technique the things to look out for are:
• good flexion of the shoulder and elbow joints. This will enable the horse to carry his knees higher over the jump
• both knees equally raised
• the ability to fold his forelegs quickly and efficiently
• the hind legs being neatly and tightly flexed together as a pair or simultaneously kicking out behind.

A rider that tips too far forward on take off makes it hard for the horse to push his forehand up.

How the horse jumps

SUSPENSION

Clearing an obstacle requires the horse to lower his head in order to raise the withers, and to tuck up and then extend the limbs. The shape the horse's head, neck and back make over a jump is called the bascule, while the arc of flight is referred to as a parabola.

Prerequisites for a perfect parabola

An ideal trajectory can be achieved by:
- an accurate, balanced, rhythmical approach
- an ideal flight path. Forces at take off determine the angle, height and width of the arc. These cannot be changed in mid air. The greater the force, the higher and wider the horse can jump
- the rider staying as close to the horse's centre of gravity as possible during the jump.

What happens during suspension

During the suspension phase the horse's body rotates around his centre of gravity. This is rather like a see-saw with the centre of gravity being the central point.
- As the hind legs leave the ground, the head and neck are lowered. This triggers the neck reflex to fold the

A horse jumping freely generally judges the distance accurately and makes a beautiful arc over the jump.

front legs, bringing the shoulders up through the action of the thoracic sling. Flexing the shoulder and elbow joints and lifting the scapulas by contraction of the trapezius, brachiocephalic and latissimus dorsi muscles will really help to lift the forelimbs to attain the height required.

- The forelegs continue to fold, bringing the weight closer to the centre of gravity thus increasing speed. The mechanics of the nuchal and supraspinous ligaments also help to raise the centre of gravity, further increasing the height.
- At this point of the jump the hind limbs are still extended.
- Just after the centre of the parabola the head and neck start to come up, bringing the centre of gravity back. This acts as a reflex to flex the hind limbs in order to clear the jump, and to extend the forelimbs in preparation for landing.
- As the forelimbs completely extend in preparation for landing, the latissimus dorsi contracts to help lift the back while the gluteals and flexor muscles flex the hips, hock and stifle to clear the jump.
- The suspension phase ends as the forefeet reach the ground.

Jumping technique

It is the correct positioning of the head and neck, both at take off and through suspension, that influences the jump and allows a scopey and stylish bascule.

The forelimbs generally have less clearance over the jump than hind limbs due to the rotation of the body axis.

When a rider gets left behind, he will often use the rein to maintain his own balance. This prevents the horse from using his head and neck correctly and makes it harder for him to make a successful jump.

TOP TIPS

- Sit still to remain in balance.
- Allow the horse plenty of rein to lower and extend his head and neck.
- Keeping your body in line with the horse and taking care not to twist, use your head and neck to look at the next fence.

How the horse jumps

LANDING

The front limbs take the full weight of the horse as it lands from the jump.

Prerequisites for a perfect landing

The head and neck must be up. This shifts the body weight back and slows down the rotation of the body axis, thus ensuring good balance on landing.

As it lands the trailing limb tends to be perpendicular to the ground

The angle of the leading limb is more acute

What happens as the horse lands

On landing after a jump:

- the trailing forelimb, which lands first in an almost vertical position, absorbs most of the impact. These forces have been estimated at up to two and a half times the body weight of the horse and results in the suspensory ligament and the deep digital flexor tendon being stretched to the extent that the fetlock often touches the ground. This is exacerbated by the fact that, as the horse lands on his heel with the toe turned upwards, additional strain is put on the navicular bone via the deep digital flexor tendon
- the leading forelimb, which closely follows the trailing forelimb, comes to earth at a more acute angle and has a longer stance phase than the trailing forelimb, which quickly rebounds off the ground

- the hind limbs are still tucked up in order to clear the jump as the forelimbs make contact with the ground. As they come to land, the thoracic sling, together with all the muscles of the forelimbs, contract eccentrically and isometrically to brace the leg and support the joints

- the landing stride is extremely short as the front legs must move quickly to be replaced by the hind limbs
- the landing phase ends as the hind feet make contact with the ground.

Trailing forelimb

In the case of a small jump, the hind legs will still be tucking up as the front feet reach the ground.

Bad landings

A misjudged take off or poor rider position usually result in a poor landing. A rider that is too far forward on landing makes it harder for the horse to remain in balance increasing the likelihood of pecking or falling. This is particularly the case if the horse is unable to slow the rate of rotation. Conversely a rider that unfolds too early may unbalance the horse and cause him to have a rail down behind.

RECOVERY

The recovery leads straight into the approach phase for the next jump, therefore it is vital to restore a good, rhythmical, three beat, balanced canter as soon as possible.

Prerequisites for a good recovery

To maximize readiness for another jumping effort:

- a balanced, steady landing leads imperceptibly in to an even, well balanced recovery phase
- it is important the rider maintains an upright, quiet position.

TOP TIPS

- Sit up and look at the next fence.
- Ensure that the getaway is straight.
- Make sure that the canter is balanced, rhythmical and collected and the horse is engaged and going forwards with impulsion.

What happens in the recovery phase

Recovery should only take one stride, but a bad jump can extend this phase, giving less preparation time for the jump that follows.

- As the horse's forefeet touch the ground they push the body up into the next canter stride thereby reversing the rotation of the body axis and allowing the hind legs to step under the body.
- The first stride after the jump is dissociated. This allows the horse to rebalance and re-establish a true canter. Following an awkward or unbalanced jump, it can sometimes take two or three strides to do this.

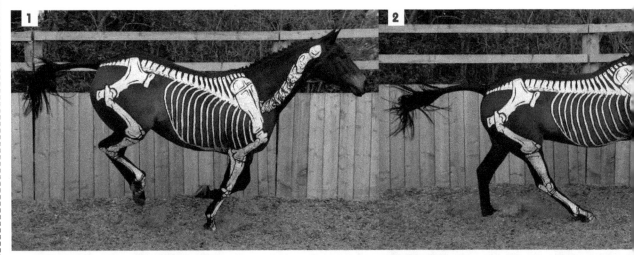

The horse uses the first stride after the jump to rebalance himself and re-establish a true three-beat canter.

Jumping a grid or a bounce

When the horse is jumping a bounce there is no get-away stride as the landing and take off strides are one and the same. This means that the forces absorbed in the forelimbs are magnified as the structures both absorb the concussive forces from landing whilst simultaneously provide the upward thrust to take off. Although a line of bounces is a good gymnastic exercise to encourage the horse to use his back and become quick thinking, it puts additional strain on the tendons, ligaments and joints.

COMMON PROBLEMS

All horses are different and all react differently. Like us their tolerance and pain thresholds vary. Some are more stoic and some more sensitive than others. The secret to detecting problems early is to know your horse well and to be conscious of the smallest change in movement or behaviour patterns. This means that action can be taken sooner rather than later.

This chapter covers:

• muscle problems

• back pain

• cold backed horses

• tendon and ligament troubles

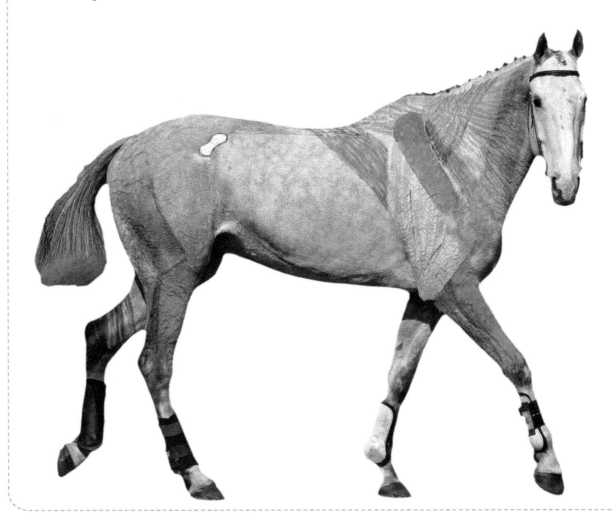

MUSCLE PROBLEMS

Muscle damage causes problems for both horse and rider. It results in ineffective, unbalanced, awkward and restricted movement, discomfort and misery. Dysfunction in any part of the dorsal or ventral chains (see pages 43–44) leads to, and is a major factor in poor performance.

Anatomy revisited

Muscles contract to create movement by applying leverage across joints. They are made up of thousands of muscle fibres called, myofibrils. Muscle activity is controlled by the nervous system, which works by sending messages around the body via nerve cells, called neurons.

> MORE THAN 60 PER CENT OF THE HORSE'S BODY WEIGHT IS MUSCLE

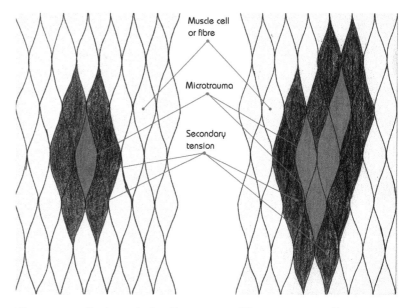

Muscle cell or fibre

Microtrauma

Secondary tension

Microtrauma affecting a single cell.   **Microtrauma spreading to adjacent muscle cells.**

What happens when muscles are damaged?

Torn fibres can cause ruptured blood vessels, bleeding, swelling and heat. This can lead to secondary muscle tension and the formation of scar tissue in the surrounding tissues. This can be a progressive process, where small numbers of fibres are injured and gradually contribute to a significant restriction of movement. This is because messages are sent from the injured area via the nervous system to the brain. It responds by sending messages to the muscles to limit movement to 'guard' the damaged area. Damage is more likely to occur during eccentric exercise, for example, when the horse suddenly stops or lands from a jump.

What causes muscle problems?

There are a number of factors that may precipitate muscle damage.

A sudden incident or accident – this can be as a result of a fall, the horse trying to stop himself going down, getting cast, or indeed any trauma or acute strain where muscle fibres are overloaded and torn.

Microtrauma – every time a muscle works there will be some wear and tear. This is normal and the muscles will usually repair when at rest.

Microtrauma is the result of just a few fibres being damaged. In the first instance the inflammation may be too small to notice. This is because not all muscle fibres are recruited simultaneously. Damaged fibres are shored up by their neighbours and activity continues. This is rather like a factory shift system where some of the labour force works whilst others rest. As more of the fibres become damaged, adjacent ones have to work harder in an ever increasing radius to make up for any deficiency until the muscle 'suddenly' becomes damaged and pain is felt. Function deteriorates as more cells come under strain and an imbalance is created within the muscle or muscle group until eventually it can affect the entire muscular system.

Overuse – this is caused by too many uninterrupted repetitions of an activity thus putting one part of the muscular skeletal system under excessive and constant strain. The immediate impact of any repetitive action or overzealous training may be negligible but, when it occurs repeatedly, the cumulative effect of constant straining causes damage.

Pulled or strained muscles – these are probably as common in the equine athlete as they are in the human. They are caused by overstretching and again result in rupture of muscle fibres.

Delayed Onset Muscle Syndrome (DOMS) – this is a type of muscle soreness that occurs after intense exercise and is characterized by mild discomfort, which can begin within a few hours of exercise and reach a maximum after 1–3 days. It is thought to be a protein breakdown as a reaction to using unaccustomed muscles. It results in cell inflammation and heat, which activate pain sensors around the muscle fibres. Delayed muscle soreness is categorized between muscle fatigue and muscle strain.

Muscle atrophy – muscle atrophy and weakness can occur as a result of interference with the nerve supply to muscles.

Muscle fatigue – muscles need enough glycogen to operate effectively. When levels fall below the amount necessary, they fatigue. Glycogen is a complex carbohydrate stored in the liver and muscles. When supplies are depleted, the muscles cannot contract efficiently and so tire easily. In humans, this is easy to cope with; we just stop exercising. The horse does not have this luxury. It is up to us to read the signs that he is tired.

The rate at which horse's muscles tire will be very different, depending on the proportion of fast to slow twitch fibre types. An endurance horse has a high number of slow twitch fibres. A sprint racer has more fast twitch fibres (see page 13).

Finesse of movement cannot co-exist with muscle fatigue.

This horse may be experiencing muscle fatigue following intense exercise.

Factors contributing to muscle problems

- Poor muscle conditioning.
- Insufficient or inappropriate warm up.
- Too much work imposed on a young, inexperienced horse without breaks.
- Ill-fitting tack.
- Imbalance related to the feet and shoeing
- Rider imbalance.

Signs and symptoms

The symptoms of muscle damage are a combination of swelling, stiffness, inflammation, soreness and heat. The less severe the symptoms, the more subtle and difficult they are to detect. Primary injury of the musculature of the back is rare. Muscle soreness in the lumbar region is commonly a secondary symptom of hind limb lameness.

Signs are:
- poor performance
- reluctance to perform moves that previously were executed with ease
- reduced stride length
- hollowing and a reluctance to go forward
- reluctance to be groomed or saddled
- a downcast demeanour.

Detecting muscle problems

Being really familiar with your horse's body can allow you to recognize the smallest of changes. These include:
- heat due to increased blood flow
- swelling from fluid accumulation
- pain on palpation or during movement
- increased tension or 'tightness'.

Regular maintenance massage is possibly the most effective way of identifying muscle tension. A therapist can often feel it long before it actually becomes a painful condition, particularly if he treats the horse on a preventative basis.

SEEK ADVICE FROM YOUR VET IF YOU SUSPECT MUSCLE DAMAGE. IF APPROPRIATE, HE CAN THEN AUTHORIZE A THERAPIST TO TREAT YOUR HORSE.

Repair

Treatment of muscle damage has two basic aims:
to promote the healing of damaged tissues
to restore full functional movement.

With any soft tissue strain, rest is vital in the early stages of recovery.

Human athletes apply the R.I.C.E. principal:
Rest – Ice – Compression – Elevation

We can hardly elevate the horse's limb, but we can follow the broad principle.

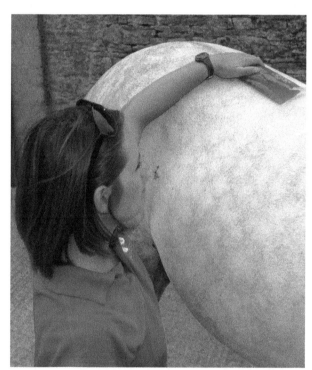

Alternatively applying heat then ice is good for muscle tears and strains.

During recovery, muscle stimulation may be a useful aid if it is used by a professional. Therapeutic ultrasound, magnetic therapy, cold laser therapy, chiropractic manipulations and acupuncture, as well as massage, are all non-invasive, may help, and can do no harm.

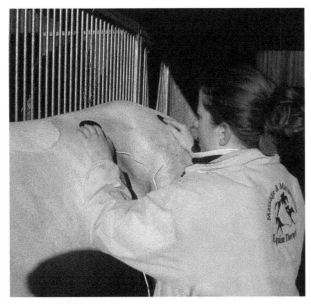

Prevention of reccurrence

Any overuse injury that has occurred once will probably recur if the same activity, or level of activity, is repeated. Avoid re-injury by changing the pattern, frequency and rest periods between activities. Keep muscles warm by using an exercise sheet if it is really cold.

Devise a massage programme or ask a therapist to show you a routine maintenance programme you can perform on your horse.

Healing muscles takes time. New muscle fibres must grow from special cells within the muscle. These must then strengthen and mature before the horse can return to the pre-injury level of work.

The use of a solarium can warm muscles, increase the circulation in the back, promote muscle tone, and reduce the build up of lactic acid.

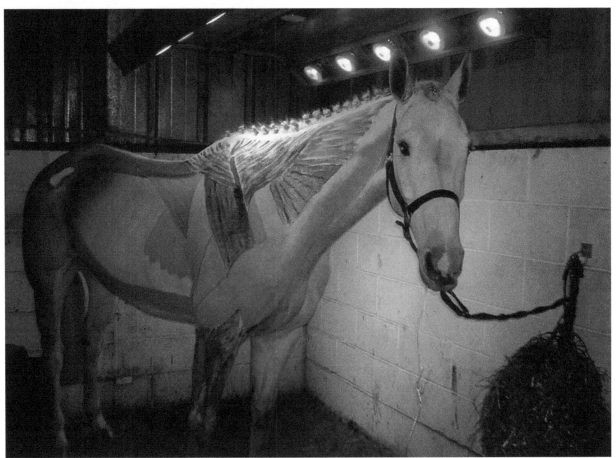

BACK PAIN

As with people, back pain in horses is frustratingly elusive to pinpoint and notoriously difficult to cure. Signs and symptoms can be numerous, variable, conflicting, and may indicate a problem elsewhere. They can also be intermittent.

Anatomy revisited

The equine back is a long, complex structure. The bones are linked by synovial facet joints and fibrous intervertebral discs. Support is provided by the supraspinous, interspinous, and the dorsal and ventral longitudinal ligaments. The longissimus dorsi together with the multifidus and other vertebral muscles move and stabilize the spine.

Some causes of back pain

There are far too many causes of back pain to list them all, but some of the most commonly encountered may be related to:

- injury, twisting, turning sharply, slipping, falling or jumping awkwardly
- conformation. Horses with long backs are susceptible to muscle and ligament strains whereas short backed horses are stronger but more prone to vertebral problems
- pain transmitted to the back from elsewhere via the muscle chains. Hind limb lameness, stemming from the hock, for example, may be a cause
- compensating for rider imbalance, which can affect the horse's musculature
- repetitive training without taking into account the age and stage of the horse
- compensating for altered movement patterns
- unbalanced feet or shoeing
- ill-fitting saddles, which can rub, cause pressure, irritate the skin or cause nerve problems.

There are many more serious reasons for back pain, such as fractures, kissing spines or arthritis. These are not within the realm of this book.

Compensating for rider imbalance is a common cause of back pain in the horse.

Signs and symptoms of back pain

Behavioural changes in your horse can indicate a problem with his back. Signs and symptoms include:

- change in temperament
- inexplicably resisting previously enjoyed activities, for example, grooming or massaging
- rolling more
- constantly resting a leg or shifting the weight when standing still
- dipping the back whilst being mounted (see page 118)
- reluctance to work
- either wanting to, or showing reluctance to, stretch the neck down
- general loss of mobility
- displaying an awkward posture or appearing stiff
- favouring one canter lead, constantly changing legs or being disunited.

You may also notice:
- areas of muscle spasm
- soreness on palpation.

Discomfort in the lumbo-sacral region

As the lumbo-sacral junction is the most flexible area of the back after the neck and tail, flexion and extension associated with jumping, galloping, and high levels of engagement, impose strain.

Due to its role in absorbing and transferring forces forward, the sacroiliac joint is prone to strain when galloping and jumping at speed.

He's not quite right!

A sensitive rider can often detect subtle differences in movement but not be able to put their finger on what is wrong. Slight changes in movement or slight underperformance can be attributable to so many causes. This makes the vet's job difficult, particularly if there is no clinical lameness or obvious discomfort. Compensatory tactics on the part of the horse can also mask the problem. The horse has the ability to change muscle recruitment in order to avoid pain, yet still comply with the rider's requirement. New movement patterns quickly become imprinted on the brain rapidly becoming the 'norm' and creating patterns that are sometimes difficult to break.

Signs in addition to some or all of the above may include:
- any form of lameness, however, mild
- reduced hind limb power and impulsion, often characterized by the inability to track up
- unequal pushing from the hind legs. This could be as a result of right or left leg dominance
- dragging the toes
- holding the tail to the affected side
- asymmetry of the tuber coxae
- muscle wasting
- unequal weight bearing on the front feet
- crooked movement.

If you suspect your horse has back pain, call your vet. He will be able to eliminate the least likely causes and advise what action to take.

How muscles compensate in horses with back pain

In horses that have weak core strength, the work of the multifidus may be replaced by that of the longissimus dorsi, which is a movement rather than a postural muscle. This causes the back to be held in a more rigid posture, resulting in stiffness and poor performance.

What to do if you suspect back pain in your horse

Once back pain has been identified and diagnosed, an appropriate course of action can be taken. It will almost certainly involve rest followed by controlled exercise.

It may include anti-inflammatory, pain relief or other prescribed medication. Manipulation, massage, heat treatment and physiotherapy can all help. Re-education is required to avoid recurrence of the problem.

TOP TIPS

- Eliminate the simple causes first. Check saddle fit and rider position.
- Train progressively, especially with young horses.
- Spend plenty of time warming up your horse in walk.
- Canter before you trot, especially if your horse is stiff.
- Attempt to identify any movements that induce back pain and take steps to avoid them.

Reflexes

A therapist will almost certainly test the horse's reflex points. The horse will react by either rounding or hollowing his back. This is similar to the 'jerk' produced when your knee is tapped. There are also reflex points, which create a sideways movement. **These are not an indication of pain**, rather the opposite – they are a natural reaction to stimuli and an indication that the muscles are functioning correctly. Be very wary of any therapist who leads you to believe they are identifying then instantly 'curing' back pain.

COLD BACKED HORSES

The term cold backed is a description of the symptoms exhibited by a horse that objects to being saddled, girthed or mounted. Reactions can vary from mild to dramatic.

Some may dip away, put the back up, stamp or 'pull faces' as a response to saddle pressure.

Once tacked up the cold backed horse may swing away as the rider attempts to mount and, once mounted may react by arching, dipping their backs or running off.

In very extreme cases the horse might throw himself to the ground. This can be very alarming and is also potentially dangerous.

Cold backed horses often demonstrate resistance.

Some will throw in a few bucks for good measure!

What are the causes?

Underneath the horse's saddle, either side of the spinous processes in the thoracic region, there is a reflex point. When stimulated, this causes the horse to involuntarily dip his back. If for some reason the weight of the rider on the saddle irritates these reflex points, the horse cannot avoid dipping his back.

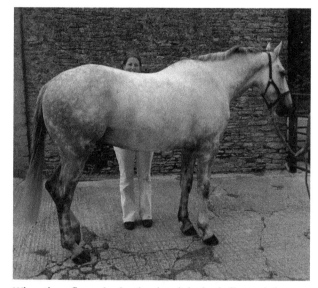

When the reflex point is stimulated the back dips and the head comes up.

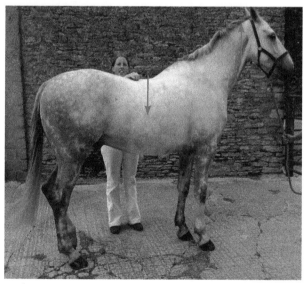

At rest.

Cold backed behaviour is thought to be related to back pain or the memory of pain. It most probably relates to discomfort in the latissimus dorsi or the thoracic portion of the trapezius muscle, but may have its origins in any part of the musculoskeletal system.

A cold backed horse tends to work normally as the affected muscles warm up, lengthen, and become accustomed to the pressure of the saddle and rider. This is not dissimilar to ourselves. If we are stiff in the mornings, this tends to wear off as we get going. It does not mean there is no underlying problem but is possibly a result of undetectable low grade back pain.

The acute reaction seen in cold-backed horses is possibly caused by the stimulation of sensitive nerve endings. This may be due to pressure from a badly fitting saddle or stretching of immobile or injured tissue. Back pain may also develop as a consequence of underlying lameness, as the horse adjusts his posture to avoid bearing weight on the affected limb.

TENDON AND LIGAMENT TROUBLES

Tendons store elastic energy, contributing to forward momentum. They are very strong structures but do not have much stretch. They act as a spring so if they are suddenly over-stretched, they can tear, and in some cases, rupture completely. The majority of problems arise in the forelimbs of horses due to additional forces applied while doing fast work or jumping.

How and where injury occurs

Any factor that increases the stress on the long vulnerable tendons running down the back of the leg can result in strain or injury.

Tendon and ligament strains and sprains are more common injuries in the lower limbs of performance than leisure horses.

Tendon damage occurs when one of the tendons or ligaments responsible for supporting the leg is torn. Although this may happen suddenly, the problem could have been building up over many months. Injury may be mild, moderate or severe; the more serious the injury, the poorer the prognosis.

The most common injuries are found in the main structures of the forelimbs which bear the brunt of the workload. They are:
- the superficial digital flexor tendon, which tends to be the most commonly damaged
- the deep digital flexor tendon
- the inferior check ligament, which is located just below the back of the knee
- the suspensory ligament.

Suspensory ligament

Situated between the deep flexor tendon and the cannon bone, this ligament differs from a tendon in that it does not have an associated muscle and is itself a modified muscle (see page 38). With regard to injury and rehabilitation, it can be considered in the same category as a tendon. Injury most often occurs as a result of over-extension of the fetlock joint.

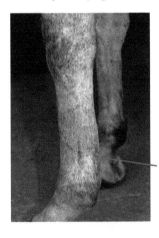

Injury to the superficial digital flexor tendon can result in a bow.

Factors that can increase the strain on tendons include:
- the relative inelasticity of the tendon compared to the parent muscle above the knee. If this muscle is damaged in any way that limits its stretch, strain on the tendon will be greater
- conformation, such as long sloping pasterns, long toes and low heels. Good farriery can help here
- any action that increases the mechanical load on the fetlock while the limb is being subjected to pressure from above and below, for example, hard uneven ground, heavy going or deep surfaces
- fatigue towards the end of a competition
- incorrect conditioning or warm up. Tendon injuries rarely happen 'suddenly'. They are often the last straw
- temperature. Cold tissues are less pliable and therefore are more susceptible to injury
- weight. Horses that are overweight or carry heavy riders put extra strain on their tendons
- degenerative ageing, which can result in weakening. This tends to occur as a result of micro-tears that have built up gradually over a period of time and can be a problem in older competition horses
- heat generated by protective leg gear. It is important to remove boots and cool the legs as quickly as possible after strenuous exercise.

Tendon troubles are complex and come in many different guises with a variety of symptoms. There can be varying degrees of heat and swelling, and lameness can be severe or non existent! There will always be pain on palpation of acute tendon strain, in other words the horse will always react if you squeeze the injured tendon.

If you suspect tendon injury, call your vet who is able to diagnose the problem more accurately and advise as to the best course of action.

TOP TIPS

- Be familiar with your horse's legs.
- Do not ignore any tendon swelling as it is often a warning sign.
- Exercise regularly.
- Avoid fast work on heavy, hard or uneven surfaces.
- Vary training regimes to avoid accumulative leg stress.
- Avoid over-tight, restrictive bandages.
- Remove boots or bandages immediately after exercise.

SUMMARY

- **Overstretching results in rupture of fibres and may be accompanied by heat, pain and swelling.**
- **Call your vet if you suspect a tendon injury. Better to be safe than sorry!**
- **The road to recovery can be long and requires a lot of patience.**

Some facts and figures

- When tendons are damaged type one 'wavy' organized collagen is replaced by type three, which is more fibrous, but less resilient. Repaired tendons have less elasticity and are therefore more susceptible to re-injury.
- When tendons overstretch to the point of damage, fibres and blood vessels will begin to rupture, usually beginning within the central core of the tendon, resulting in the inflammation, pain and swelling of a 'bowed' tendon.
- An ultrasound examination is used to assess the structure and degree of damage to the tendon or ligament.
- Inflammation of a ligament is known as desmitis.
- Treatment will initially involve box rest, cold application, use of support bandages, anti-inflammatories, then at least three months of gradual controlled exercise. Tendon scans are used to assess progress before exercise levels are increased. You will be guided by your vet.

TROUBLESHOOTING

Keeping the musculoskeletal system in optimum condition is a priority in the prevention and treatment of problems. Sports medicine focuses on physical fitness and includes exercise regimes, massage, stretching, core strengthening exercises, correct preparation and cool down, all of which help to keep your horse physically supple and toned. It is an important weapon in the armoury against injury.

This chapter covers:

• conditioning muscles

• Pilates for horses

• ...and riders

• massage and muscular manipulation

• how to massage

• stretching for horses

CONDITIONING MUSCLES

Well toned, supple muscles can stretch and contract freely. To avoid injury, it is important for a horse to be fit for the work he does, and for him to be adequately warmed up and cooled down.

The dangers of tight muscles

Short, tight muscles put strain on sites of origin and insertion, pulling on the joints and tendons and leading to an increased susceptibility to injury.

Muscular damage, in addition to being painful and debilitating for the horse, requires a lengthy and often costly recovery and rehabilitation period. It is prudent therefore to take steps to avoid damage. Correct stretching and warm up is an effective way of preventing muscle and ligament damage.

Tight shortened muscles are a contributory factor in tendon injuries, which are the most common soft tissue injury in the performance horse. When the muscles are tight, overstretch injuries easily occur.

The distance from a muscle's point of origin to the point of insertion in the lower limb is designed to cover an exact distance. When muscles become tight, it is more difficult for them to extend fully and so the less flexible tendons are put under strain.

Torn or strained muscles can be a result of a stretch that takes the muscle beyond its physiological limits.

Exercise increases the amount of flexibility around a joint, whilst decreasing the amount of resistance.

Flexibility

Flexibility refers to the range of movement in and around a joint. It depends on many interrelated factors the most relevant of which is the length and elasticity of the muscles and ligaments. Flexibility is influenced by temperature. Both muscles and joints are more flexible when body temperature is raised by 1 or 2°C.

Flexibility can also be increased by regular mobilization of the muscles either by performing specific exercises or, by taking the joints statically or dynamically through their full range of movement.

Suppleness

This is the ability to achieve a full range of movement without stiffness, restriction or discomfort. When riding our horses it is this suppleness, flexibility, elasticity and ease of movement that we are trying to achieve.

Lengthening of muscles is the goal in working towards optimum suppleness. Human athletes continually work on stretching, suppling and elongating muscles (see pages 134–135). The horse will benefit from the same process.

In hand exercises are a good way to increase suppleness.

A supple horse will step through well, be able to perform lateral movements with ease, and bend comfortably to the right and left.

Improving muscle tone

Building muscle strength and flexibility is an important part of training. Strong, well-toned muscles protect against musculoskeletal injury by stabilizing joints and reducing the strain on tendons and ligaments. For a muscle to improve in tone and strength, it must undergo activity that stimulates more than 75 per cent of the muscle fibres in maximum tension. Low-intensity exercise increases endurance while jumping or working at speed recruits most fibres, causing them to grow and increase in strength.

TOP TIPS

- Train regularly. Shorter, more intense exercise several times a week increases muscular condition more effectively than a longer period once a week.
- Train appropriately. For activities that require strength or power, such as jumping, fewer repetitions performed at higher intensity are effective. For disciplines that require less power but more stamina, for example, dressage or endurance, less-intense exercise, with a greater number of repetitions are appropriate.
- The same type of exercise should not be performed day after day. Plan a varied programme. This activates more muscle groups and allows tissues time to recover. Intersperse school work with hacking, cross training, hill work, jumping, and fast work.
- As horses move up the fitness ladder muscle conditioning may need to be more specific.

PILATES FOR HORSES

Pilates is a conditioning system that increases core stability, strength and body awareness; redresses imbalances, and realigns the body from the inside out. It can improve posture, achieve a balance between strength and flexibility, and relieve tension. It is popular with Olympic athletes and sportspeople from all disciplines.

Developed by Joseph Pilates, an authority on movement and biomechanics, he continually developed and refined a programme of exercises and stretches based on the principal that a strong core supports the back and minimizes the risk of muscular damage.

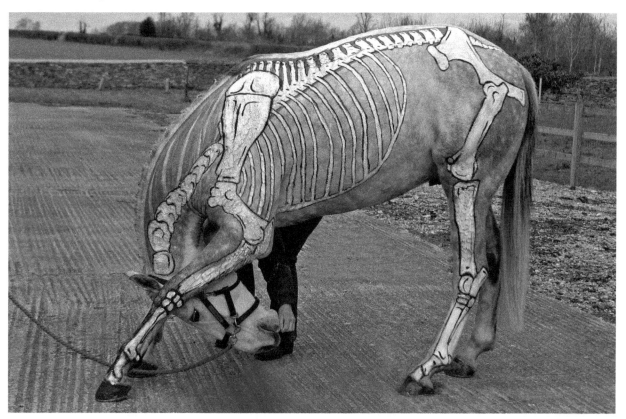

Practise makes perfect!

Core stability exercises for horses

Many of the Pilates principles can be applied to the horse. By performing specific stretch exercises, the core muscles that make the back strong and assist in carrying the weight of the rider can be strengthened. These include the deep internal muscles of the abdomen, pelvis, thoracic sling, and back together with the more superficial muscles of the trunk.

Neutral Spine, a key feature in Pilates, is the natural position of the spine when all body parts are in good alignment. In horses this translates to correct alignment of the vertebrae and correct spinal curves forming a strong bridge, relieving pressure on the back and allowing movement to become fluid and free.

Performing core stability exercises helps to keep the equine athlete strong, supple and injury free. These exercises are active, where the horse uses his own muscles to move his body or reach for a reward, such as carrot.

The more proficient the horse becomes, the greater the benefit. For core stability exercises to have an impact, they must be performed regularly four to five times a week over a period of about three months. For benefits to accrue they must then be practised regularly at least three times a week. Where appropriate, they must be performed equally to both sides.

IF YOU SUSPECT ANY MUSCULAR SKELETAL PROBLEMS, CHECK WITH YOUR VET BEFORE EMBARKING ON ANY STRETCHING PROGRAMME.

Troubleshooting

Exercise one – carrot between front legs

Aim
• To lift and flex the withers, neck and back. To increase core stability, the musculature of the top line, abdominal strength and back flexibility.

This exercise is equivalent to our sit ups.

How to do it
• Using a carrot, encourage the horse to bring his head down then back between his front legs.
• Keep the carrot close to the lips to discourage 'bounce'.
• Hold the stretch for 5–10 seconds before allowing the horse to take the carrot.
• Repeat 2–3 times per session gradually increasing the stretch by taking the head further back.

Good for
• Flexing the base of the neck and lifting the back by stimulating the abdominal muscles.
• Promoting correct posture and support for the back.

Thoracic sling muscles contract to lift chest and flex the cervio-thoracic junction

Muscles through the neck, withers and back are stretched

Flexion at the base of the neck and through the cervico-thoracic junction

Flexion of the thoraco-lumbar spine region

Pelvis tilts as iliopsoas muscles are recruited

Abdominal muscles contract to lift the back

Some horses may try to cheat by bending a front leg to reach the carrot, however, as long he still contracts his abdominal muscles and lifts his back this is not a problem

Part three

Exercise two – carrot low to the side

Aim
- To lift and flex the spine to the side, and flex the base of the neck.
- To increase core stability, abdominal strength, back flexibility and suppleness.

This exercise is equivalent to our sideways sit ups.

How to do it
- Stand with your back against the horse's ribs level with the girth line.
- Holding the carrot in the hand closest to the tail, encourage the horse to bring his head across your body.
- Bring the carrot down to just below your knee. Keep the carrot close to the horse's lips to keep the movement smooth.
- Hold the stretch for 5–10 seconds before allowing the horse to take the carrot.
- Repeat 2–3 times per session gradually increasing the stretch by taking the head further back.
- As the exercise becomes easier stand nearer the tail.

Good for
- Improving suppleness through the base of the neck and the back.
- Supporting the correct posture of the back.
- Improving the ability to bend.

TOP TIPS
- You can perform this exercise in the stable.
- Always maintain a contact between your back and his ribs.

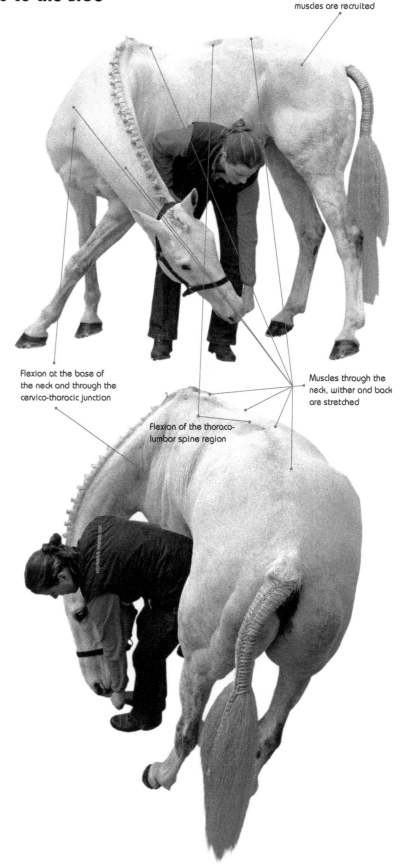

Pelvis tilts as iliopsoas muscles are recruited

Flexion at the base of the neck and through the cervico-thoracic junction

Muscles through the neck, wither and back are stretched

Flexion of the thoraco-lumbar spine region

Troubleshooting

Exercise three – backing up

Aim

• To lift and flex the back.
• To strengthen the muscles and structures involved in engagement and carrying the weight of the rider.
• To stimulate the sacroiliac area.

This is collection in reverse!

How to do it

• Walk the horse forwards into a positive halt.
• By applying gentle pressure on the chest and head collar encourage the horse to step back. As the horse becomes practised at this exercise less pressure will be required.
• Keep the head as low as possible to encourage the back to raise. If the horse has a tendency to hollow, use a carrot during this exercise to encourage him to keep his head low. Try to avoid the horse coming backwards with rushed, short, hollow steps.
• Begin with 2–3 quality steps gradually increasing to up to 10.

Good for

• Flexion of the lumbo-sacral and stimulating the sacroiliac region.

TOP TIP

• Incorporate this exercise into your daily regime by backing your horse up before you ride.

Relaxed back lifts to allow hind legs to step under

Muscles of the topline are correctly recruited

Keep the head and neck low

Pelvis tilts, lumbo-sacral junction flexes and iliopsoas muscles contract

The muscles that usually bring the leg through the swing phase now have to work in the pushing phase of the stride

Long marching steps backwards

Abdominal muscles contract to lift back

Exercise four – walking over a raised pole

Aim
- To lift and flex the back, hip, shoulder and elbow, stifle and hock.
- To strengthen the muscles and structures involved in engagement, hip flexion and pelvic stability.
- To improve suppleness and flexibility through the shoulder and elbow, hip, stifle and hock.

How to do it
- Slowly walk the horse over a pole on the ground
- Gradually raise it until it is around knee height.
- Encourage the horse to lower his head to look at the pole.

- This exercise can be performed in hand or ridden.
- Perform on a daily basis.

Good for
- Improving suppleness and flexibility through the shoulder and elbow, hip, stifle and hock.

TOP TIP
- Place a raised pole in a location where the horse can regularly walk over it; for example to and from the field.

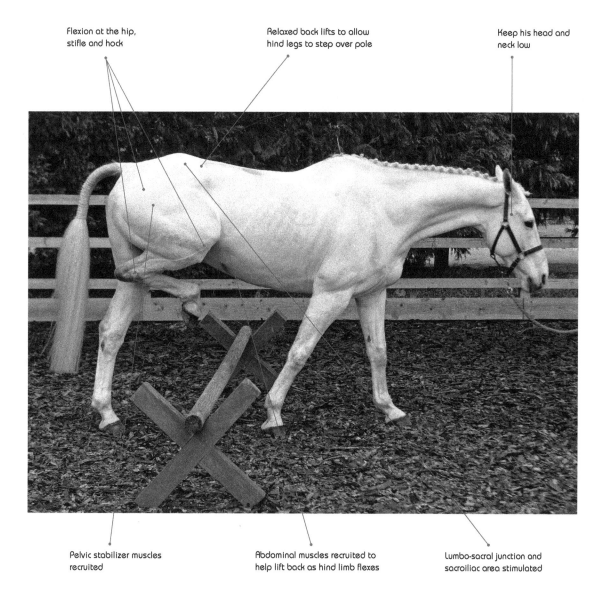

Flexion at the hip, stifle and hock

Relaxed back lifts to allow hind legs to step over pole

Keep his head and neck low

Pelvic stabilizer muscles recruited

Abdominal muscles recruited to help lift back as hind limb flexes

Lumbo-sacral junction and sacroiliac area stimulated

Troubleshooting

Exercise five – walking obliquely over a raised pole

Aim
- To lift and flex the back, hip, shoulder and elbow, stifle and hock.
- To strengthen the muscles and structures involved in engagement, hip flexion and pelvic stability.
- To improve suppleness and flexibility through the shoulder and elbow, hip, stifle and hock.
- To strengthen the muscles involved in both abduction and adduction.

How to do it
- Begin with a pole on the ground.
- Gradually raise it until it is around knee height.

- Walk diagonally across the pole encouraging the horse to keep his head low.
- Gradually decrease the angle of approach.
- This exercise can be performed in hand or ridden.
- Perform on a daily basis.

Good for
- Improving suppleness and range of movement in the joints and muscles involved in lateral exercises.

TOP TIP

- Perform this exercise on both reins.

Hip joints rotate to allow adduction and abduction of the hind limbs as the muscles work

Relaxed back lifts to allow hind legs to step over pole

Abdominal muscles recruited

Flexion at the hip, stifle and hock

Thoracic sling is stretched to allow adduction and abduction of the forelimbs

Head and neck are kept low

Part three

Exercise six – spinning

Aim

- To create lateral bend throughout the horse's body and to encourage adduction of the inside hind leg.

How to do it

- Stand the horse on a non-slip surface.
- Stand facing the horse at the girth line. Hold the lead rope in the hand nearest the head leaving the other hand free to encourage movement of the hind legs.
- Encourage the horse to walk on in a small circle around you, bending his head to the inside. Do not allow him to step backwards.
- Gently touch the horse's inside hind leg just as it leaves the ground to encourage it to step further across under his body.

Good for

- Improving suppleness, bend and lateral movements.

TOP TIPS

- This exercise requires a certain amount of skill and practise from both horse and handler. Perform on a daily routine to improve the quality of the steps.
- Perform this exercise equally on both reins.

Muscles on the inside of the bend are recruited. Neck, thoracic and lumbar vertebrae are flexed

Abdominal muscles are recruited as the inside hind leg steps under the body

The hips rotate as the hind limbs adduct and abduct

Muscles of the neck and back on the outside of the bend are stretched

Abdominal muscles are recruited as the inside hind leg steps under the body

The barrel of the ribs rotates to the outside of the bend

Thoracic sling muscles are stimulated as the forelimbs adduct and abduct

Troubleshooting

Exercise seven – reflexes

Aim
- There are a number of reflex points which, when stimulated, can be used to move the horse's back.

A WORD OF WARNING!
SOME HORSES DO NOT LIKE THESE EXERCISES AND MAY KICK. ONLY PERFORM THEM IF YOU HAVE CONFIDENCE IN YOUR HORSE.

How to do them

Sternum lift
- Stand facing the girth line.
- Stroke the horse's sternum until he becomes comfortable with your touch.
- Apply upward pressure using your finger tips. The horse should appear to come up just behind the withers.

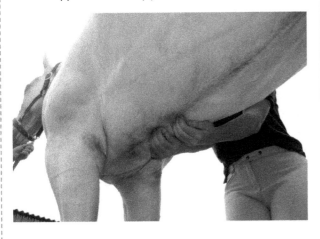

Back lift
There are two ways of achieving this reflex movement. Different horses favour different methods.

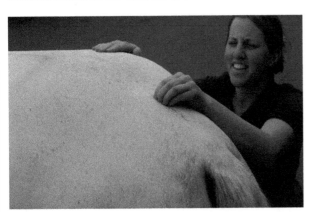

Method one.

Method one
- Stand to the side of the horse facing his hindquarters.
- Stroke the top of his tail to relax him.
- Starting at the top of the tail and working towards the head, apply gentle downward pressure from your fingertips or thumbs to each caudal vertebra in turn.
- With each application of pressure the horse should increasingly lift and round his back.
- Hold the position for a few seconds at the point of maximum flexion.

Method two
- Stand slightly to the side of the hindquarters.
- Using your fingertips, gently scratch from the top of the hindquarters, positioning one hand either side of the spine, down the back of the hind legs. This should result in the horse arching his back.

Note: this can be too irritable for sensitive horses.

Method two.

TOP TIPS

- Ensure the horse is relaxed.
- Be constantly aware of your horse's reaction.

Good for
- Improving suppleness and flexibility of the back.
- Stimulating the thoracic sling and abdominal muscles, which are important in maintaining correct posture.

The result of the back lift reflex – method one. Compare the position of the back before and during the lift.

Head and neck lowers in response to the back movement

Flexion of the thoraco-lumbar spine

Flexion of the lumbo-sacral junction

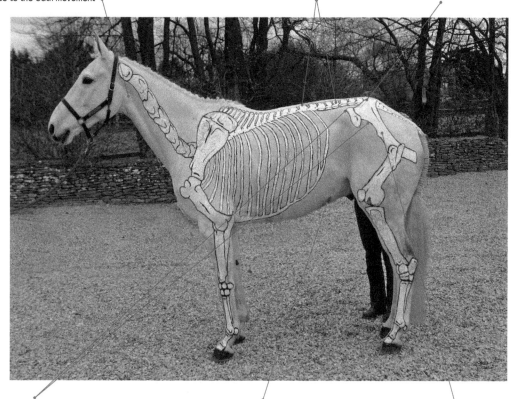

Iliopsoas muscles are recruited

Abdominal muscles contract to lift the back

Pelvis tilts

Troubleshooting

... AND RIDERS

To do justice to our equine athlete, we need to keep ourselves in good shape – consider your own fitness. Walk the last half mile home!

No matter how well we understand the way that our horses move, how well we look after their musculoskeletal systems and how well we attend to their nutritional needs, we cannot do them justice unless we keep our bodies in good order too.

To ride well, probably the most important prerequisite is good core stability. Our postural muscles, like those of the horse, need to be able to hold and maintain our position. We need good posture and balance.

Pilates builds core strength, suppleness, flexibility, grace and balance, as well as improving general body awareness.

To ride well and achieve perfect balance the rider must sit in such a way that each part of the body rests on the part directly below it. This minimizes discomfort to the horse and gives the rider the ability to ride in harmony with ease and efficiency.

Challenge your balance

Stand on one leg. Close your eyes and try not to wobble!

TOP TIP

- Enrol at a Pilates class. Even if your time is limited, the benefits are worth their weight in gold!

A general Pilates programme will develop or correct postural alignment, core strength and balance, and can have a significant influence our effectiveness as riders. A good teacher is a must until you grasp the basic principles, then the only requirements are self motivation and self determination. The rewards are a feeling of grace, harmony and relaxation. As with the horse, tension and good performance do not go hand in hand!

Activate your core

- Stand tall with the shoulders relaxed and down.
- Draw your shoulder blades down your back.
- Lengthen your neck upwards.
- Imagine that your head is being gently pulled up by a large balloon.
- Imagine you are wearing a belt. Use your muscles to pull it up really tight. Let it out half way. Try to hold it there – all the time.

Repeat this procedure, whenever you think of it, until it becomes second nature.

MASSAGE AND MUSCULAR MANIPULATION

Massage is the manipulation of soft tissues for therapeutic purposes. It is not a new concept and has been practised in China for thousands of years. It has stood the test of time. It is a hands-on technique which, by exerting external pressure, can influence the structures below. It has both a psychological and physiological effect. To gain maximum benefit it is necessary to look at the horse as a whole. Muscle tension is transmitted from one muscle group to another so areas of tension may be far removed from the site of the pain. Before embarking on massage it is advantageous to have a thorough understanding of anatomy (see pages 9–39).

The body systems that benefit

The main body structures that are affected by massage therapy include the:
- muscular system
- circulatory system
- lymphatic system
- nervous system
- skin

All the systems work together. Massage can influence the deeper, more internal structures through the circulatory and nervous systems.

The circulatory system – carries nutrients around the body. Arteries deliver the nutrients and oxygenated blood to the tissues. Veins return the oxygen-depleted blood back to the heart and lungs. Waste is filtered from the blood as it passes through the kidneys.

Venous blood is returned to the heart by movement of the muscle groups surrounding the veins. Decreased muscle activity will result in a decreased flow of venous return.

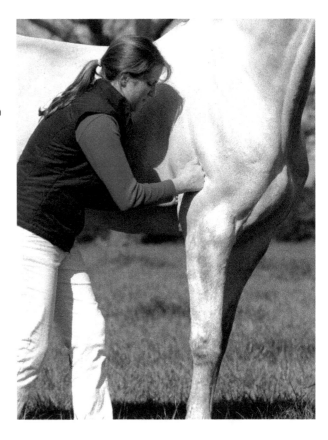

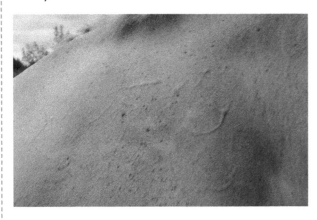

The lymphatic system – is responsible for removing excess fluid and fatty acids from body tissues and fighting infection. It is the body's first line of defence. Lymph originates from blood plasma, leaking out of vessels and into intercellular spaces, becoming tissue fluid. This fluid is eventually squeezed into lymph vessels and from there into the circulatory system leading to the heart. Reduced muscle activity will ultimately slow down lymphatic circulation.

The nervous system – controls every bodily function. The central nervous system consists of the brain and spinal cord and the peripheral nervous system consists of sensory and motor nerves. Sensory nerves carry information from the body to the central nervous system while motor nerves carry messages in the other direction. Nerve endings are influenced by massage.

Exercise increases circulation. This can sometimes be seen as raised veins in the skin. Massage also increases the circulation in an area by increasing the temperature. If an area is massaged for five minutes this will increase the surface temperature by 1°C.

When to massage

Massage is versatile! In can be used:

- as part of a daily routine. Horsemen have used it inadvertently for years as they strapped their horses
- as part of a pre- and post-exercise regime. It is especially beneficial pre- and post-competition
- in response to muscle discomfort
- as part of a recovery programme following injury or illness as directed by your vet.

> THERAPISTS SHOULD BE ABLE TO DETECT SIGNS OF MICRO-TRAUMA. OVERUSE INJURIES CAN BE REVERSIBLE, GIVEN THE CORRECT EARLY TREATMENT.

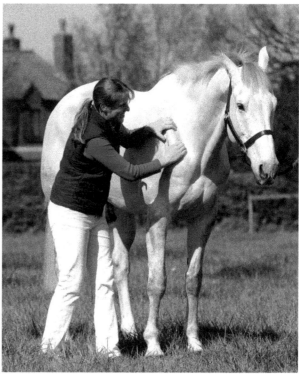

Massage promotes mental and physical relaxation via the nervous system and helps create a bond between you and your horse.

Why massage?

Massage therapy can be used to treat a specific problem or injury or to maintain the health of the soft tissues and thus prevent future problems by keeping the body balanced, and supple.

Being familiar with how your horse feels will allow you to be aware of any problems earlier rather than later. **Please note that is illegal to massage a horse other than your own without the permission of the vet** (Veterinary Surgeons Act 1966).

Massage can:

- help to relieve pain, muscle tension and any post exercise soreness
- help to improve performance and increase the range of movement
- depending on the type of massage (see page 138), relax or stimulate the muscles
- aid waste product removal via the lymphatic system
- increase blood flow, nutrient and oxygen delivery via the circulatory system
- help reduce post-exercise soreness
- breakdown scar tissue.

TOP TIP

- Have a sports and remedial massage regularly yourself. A good therapist will often be able to point out muscle tension or reduced flexibility of which you were previously unaware. Most good equine sports massage therapists are also fully qualified to treat humans. It makes sense to use someone that treats both horses and riders as they understand the muscles involved in riding and can often pinpoint imbalance between you and your horse. You will also appreciate what your horse may be feeling when he has a massage!

HOW TO MASSAGE

Equine Massage Therapy has its origins in Swedish massage, which uses a variety of different movements for different purposes. These either soothe or stimulate.

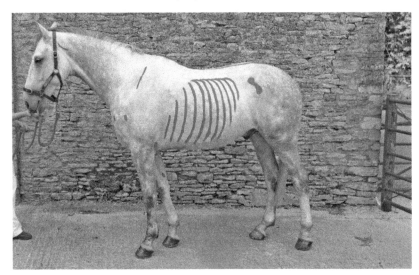

Areas to avoid: do not massage the ribs, abdomen, underside of the neck, on top of the spinous processes or any bony areas.

Effleurage is a relaxing stroking technique. It can be performed using varying degrees of pressure with both hands at the same time or in a continuous motion one after the other. Its main effect is to promote the drainage of fluids within the venous and lymphatic circulations.

Effleurage.

Petrissage is a compressive, kneading, squeezing or wringing technique performed with both hands. It produces a pumping type action by alternating pressure and relaxation. Its main effect is to mobilize tissue and improve circulation. It is important not to let your hands slip over the skin.

Petrissage.

Friction is a circular compressive technique performed with the fingers or thumbs on smaller muscles in a localized area. It assists in the breaking down of scar tissue and tension. As with petrissage, it is important not to let your hands slip.

Friction.

Tapotement is a percussive bouncing movement performed on large muscles. It directly affects the nerves and has a stimulating effect. Old fashioned strapping has similar effects. There are two main ways of performing tapotement:

• **clapping**, in which the hands are cupped, so as not to slap, and are rapidly and alternately applied to the skin. Wrists remain relaxed, producing a hollow sound. This is a mildly stimulating technique

Clapping.

• **hacking**, which involves using the sides of the hands to stimulate the skin, nerves and underlying muscle mass. It is really important to keep the wrists, hands and fingers loose so as to avoid chopping!

Hacking.

When not to massage

Do not massage:
• if a horse has a skin condition. You should also avoid any cuts and bruises
• if a horse is very lame and you do not know the cause
• if a horse is suffering from any type of infection
• if a horse has tied up
• if you are unsure for _any_ reason.

How often and how long?

Massage is best performed by a skilled and trained therapist who will be able to assess your horse's musculature and plan an appropriate programme. They will demonstrate the techniques you can use between treatments.
• The most basic form of massage is grooming. This can be done energetically on a daily basis.
• If your horse is recovering from injury, a massage routine up to three times a week is beneficial.
• Once a week is helpful for mild problems.
• Once a month is useful for maintenance and early detection of problems.
• A complete massage can take anything up to an hour and a half.

TOP TIPS

• Both you and your horse need to be in a relaxed frame of mind.
• Think about your own posture while you are massaging. Use your weight rather than your strength.
• Stand on a box in order to get your weight behind the techniques.
• Practise on a friend first. They can give you some feedback!
• Perform all techniques smoothly, evenly and rhythmically.

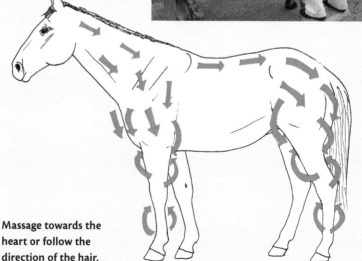

Massage towards the heart or follow the direction of the hair.

Troubleshooting

STRETCHING FOR HORSES

Human athletes have long understood the benefits of stretching, especially relative to improving athletic ability and performance. Horses can also reap the benefits if performed correctly on a regular basis.

Why stretch?

The main objective of successful training is to achieve the best possible performance while keeping the horse injury free. To do this requires a healthy musculature so, maintaining flexibility and suppleness is an important factor in reducing the risk of muscle or tendon damage.

Vets and therapists are becoming increasingly aware of the advantages of stretching and many sports therapists perform stretching as part of their treatment.

Stretching is an important aspect of elongating the muscle fibres. It can:
• increase the range of movement, flexibility, athleticism and suppleness
• reduce muscular soreness, tension and stiffness
• reduce the risk of injury to joints, muscles and tendons
• improve coordination
• maintain the current level of flexibility
• increase mental and physical relaxation
• increase circulation
• enhance body awareness.

Types of stretching

There are two main types of stretching:

- **passive stretches** are performed by a handler. The horse needs to be relaxed and confident to achieve these stretches

- **active stretches** require active muscle contraction from the horse to move body parts and create the stretch himself. Active stretches can be performed during ridden or groundwork exercises, and also with the use of a reward, such as a carrot, to stretch the neck.

How to start

Take advice from a therapist, she will assess your horse's musculature and plan a suitable programme of stretches. She will also show you how to perform them safely without risk to either you or your horse.

Begin slowly. Once the maximum stretch is reached, hold it there for 5–15 seconds to allow the fibres to relax before taking the stretch a little further.

TOP TIPS

- It is absolutely vital that the horse is warm. Never attempt to stretch cold muscles.
- Work a manageable programme into your daily routine.
- Be patient. You will only see the benefits of stretching if you perform the stretches regularly and consistently.

Physiology of stretching

The stretching of a muscle fibre begins with contraction of the sarcomeres, which makes the thick and thin myobifils elongate. Once the muscle fibre has reached its maximum resting length, taking the stretch that little bit further allows the collagen fibres in the connective tissue to stretch and realign in the same direction as the tension. It is this realignment as a result of stretching that extends the muscle length.

The spindle reflex

Muscle spindles are found within the belly of the muscle and run parallel to the main muscle fibres. When the muscle is stretched, so too is the muscle spindle, which reacts by sending information about action (via its sensory nerve supply) to the central nervous system. When a stretch is held for any length of time it, is the spindle that imprints the new length on the central nervous system. In this way the muscle spindle contributes to muscle tone and protects the body from injury.

PRACTICAL CONSIDERATIONS

Of course we all want the best for, and to get the best from, our horses. After all, we invest a lot of time and energy in them! Avoiding some of the heartache caused when things go wrong has got to be useful. Whatever your aspiration, whether it is to win a competition or to enjoy fun rides, it is definitely advantageous to be aware of the ideal surroundings for your horse. This chapter looks at some ways of recognizing and managing their environment for optimum benefit. There is also advice about conformation that optimizes good movement.

This chapter covers:

• stable management for a happy and healthy horse

• anatomy for movement

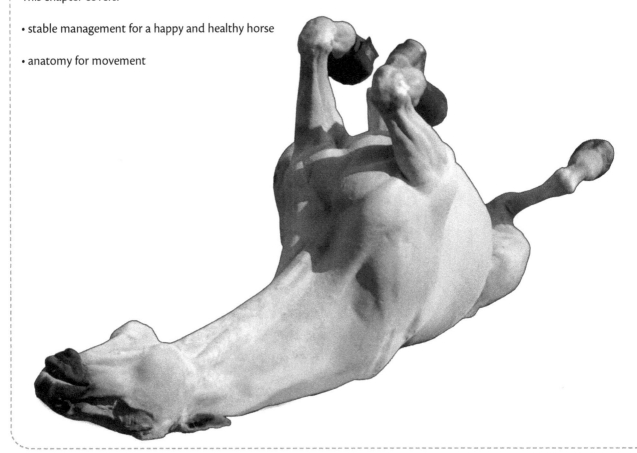

STABLE MANAGEMENT FOR A HAPPY AND HEALTHY HORSE

The best environment for the horse is one that mimics his natural environment as closely as possible. The best place for a horse is in the field where he can give rein to natural behaviour. This is good for him both mentally and physically. Many stable vices can be attributed to boredom. Because many horses are kept at livery, it is not always possible to keep your horse in the manner you would like. However, it pays to try and achieve the best possible conditions for your horse to keep him happy and healthy.

Tips for a happy, healthy horse

Postural work begins with the way a horse is tied, fed, groomed, led, mounted and ridden and so paying close attention to these areas can bring big benefits your horse.

In the stable

- Feed hay, concentrates and water from floor level. There are numerous reasons for this:
  - it ensures the back is held in the correct position and maintains correct alignment through the cervical and thoracic vertebrae as the ligaments of the neck and back come into play. Consider the length of time the horse might stand eating with his head held unnaturally high and his back hollowed. This puts unnecessary strain on the musculoskeletal system
  - it stimulates the muscles and structures involved in supporting the back and carrying the weight of the rider, so it helps prepare a young horse for work
  - it is better for the horse's respiration as mucus is assisted by gravity in removing dust from the air passages out through the nostrils,
  - it is better for the digestion of the horse and production of saliva
  - it enables efficient use of the chewing mechanism.
- As the horse is a trickle feeder, provide ad lib hay wherever possible. Failing this, feeding little and often is best. Feeding in this way allows a steady production of saliva, which neutralizes stomach acid. Horses that are fed twice a day are subjected to prolonged periods without feed to neutralize the acid; an empty stomach is much more prone to ulcers. It has been estimated that around 90 per cent of racehorses, 60 per cent of competition horses and 50 per cent of stabled leisure horses suffer from gastric ulcers. Left untreated, they can cause a variety of signs ranging from weight loss and poor performance to recurrent colic.
- Place a brick in the feed bowl to slow down eating.

Eating in this position is bad for the back and causes uneven wear patterns in the teeth.

Feeding from the floor in the natural position is good for the back and neck, maintains clear sinuses, and is good for the respiratory and digestive systems.

- Provide a variety of different types of hay in all corners of the stable, both for nutritional variety and to encourage the horse to move around and mimic natural foraging patterns.
- Feed a balanced diet. Take advice from a feed company regarding the best feeding regime for the level of work.
- Place a lick on the floor to provide essential nutrients.
- Provide stable toys, for example, a ball that dispenses food, to relieve boredom.

- Horses are gregarious herd animals so ensure that your horse can see other horses.
- Leave the stable door open with a chain across it during the day. Horses often doze with their head over the door. A chain allows the head to sink lower, which is better for the back.

- Beware of stable doors that are too high for small ponies. It can cause them to adopt an unnaturally high head carriage, which may affect their posture as they try to peer over it.

The horse's stomach

To understand why ulcers occur, it is necessary to be aware of how the stomach works.

The horse's stomach is very acidic and contains enzymes to digest proteins. To protect itself against the acid, the wall of the stomach produces a mucus lining. Saliva, only produced when the horse is chewing, also helps to neutralize the acid. Ulcers occur when the acid in the stomach is greater than the protective factors. These erosions in the wall of the stomach are caused literally by the stomach 'digesting' itself.

The stomach is divided into two parts. The lower part is glandular, tougher, and has cells that produce protective mucus. Because it is lower, the contents are normally submerged. Ulcers are less likely to be found there. The top part is the most common place to find ulcers, which occur when the acid production exceeds the protective factors or when during exercise the acidic contents of the lower stomach are splashed on to the upper part. Thus, horses in hard work, or who are travelled, have insufficient fibre in the diet, or are left in the stable for periods without food are more susceptible.

The horse's stomach

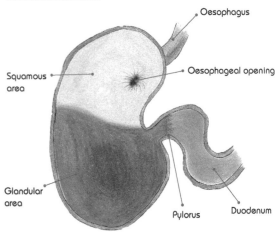

If you suspect gastric ulcers call the vet who will advise on the best course of action.

- Wrap metal bars over stable doors in insulating materials to soften the blow if the horse should throw his head up.
- Ensure the floor is flat, especially where the horse stands. A dip near the door can causes the forelimbs to be unevenly loaded.
- Fit rubber stable mats to reduce jar from a concrete floor. If this is not possible at least place a strip of flooring across the doorway and where the horse stands to feed.

- Ensure a comfortable, clean bed. This can also prevent injuries when the horse gets up.
- Fit the stable with anti cast strips. Horses, once cast, can do themselves immeasurable damage, particularly to the pelvic and hip region. Strips allow them grip and leverage on the wall and can help them to get back on their feet.
- Groom every day. This forms a psychological bond with the horse, allows you to notice and respond to any changes, and, particularly if it includes strapping, tones the muscles.

In the yard

- Avoid situations where the horse pulls back or panics when tied up as this can cause considerable damage to the poll area.
- Ensure he is safely tied with a material that will snap.
- Tying the head too high is not good for the back.
- Lead the horse equally from both sides to help maintain straightness. This also applies to mounting.
- Use a mounting block whenever possible to prevent continual strain on the muscles and back.

Travelling

Travelling is stressful. Anything that can be done to alleviate both stress and muscle tension, is a good thing. Ensure that:

- there is enough space for the horse to get his head down and spread his legs to keep his balance whilst travelling. Travelling long distances with the head high puts strain on the back
- the horse has access to haylage to keep the stomach full
- he is well protected with boots, tail bandages and a poll guard
- the box or trailer is long enough for the horse
- on long journeys you plan time for regular breaks so the horse can stretch his legs, have a drink and get his head down to graze.

Teeth

Horse's teeth are designed to chew for 16–18 hours a day. They are open rooted, grow throughout life and are capable of dealing with much tougher forage than we feed today. The stable horse tends not to use his teeth for as long as this, the consequence of which can be dental overgrowth that can affect eating and performance.

Horses chew in a side to side motion. This ensures even wear on the teeth and maximum production of saliva. They can only do this when their heads are in a natural grazing position. Eating from high racks or nets produces a different rotation which can also lead to the development of hooks and sharp edges. Another good reason to feed hay from the floor.

A horse that is uncomfortable in the mouth will do his best to evade the bit. This will lead to resistance. Tension in the jaw will also affect flexion at the poll and the correct positioning of the head and neck.

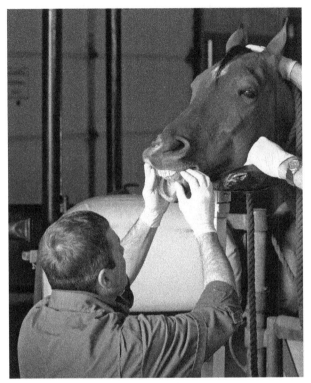

Have your horse's teeth checked regularly; every 6 months is advisable. Ensure that your dentist is fully qualified and recognized by the British Equine Veterinary Association.

Saddlery

This is an area for a qualified saddle fitter recognized by the Society of Master Saddlers. It is important that the saddle fit both horse and rider. A few key points that the saddler will look for that relate to anatomy are:
- the tree must be the correct size for the horse
- the saddle must not interfere with the action of the horse's scapula
- the saddle must be fitted in such a way that the rider sits in the centre of the horse's movement
- there should be no pressure points
- the saddle must remain centrally located at all paces and be free from excessive movement, such as swinging, swaying, rocking and rotating
- all aspects of the saddle must be symmetrical or correctly adjusted for any muscular imbalances or one-sidedness
- it is important that all saddles are checked regularly as the horse continually changes shape over the year and the flocking within the saddle will gradually settle.

Numnahs

It is important that the numnah is clean to prevent chafing, and fits the saddle. A correctly shaped, high wither numnah is best as a flat 'blanket' type can pull tight and restrict the withers.

The 'blanket' type numnah.

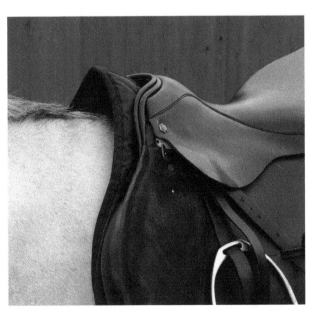

The high wither numnah.

Bits

It is important to use a well fitting bit in order to protect the delicate bars of the mouth and to encourage saliva production and swallowing. The horse must be as comfortable as possible in his mouth, so he can be relaxed and concentrate on what the rider is asking him to do.

The main reason that the horse resists the bit, is to escape either pain or pressure on the tongue, which prevents swallowing. To feel this sensation yourself, press your finger on your tongue and try and swallow.

If in doubt about the best type of bit for your horse, enlist the help of a qualified trainer or bitting specialist.

Emotional well being

Like us, horses can become stressed and this can manifest itself in tension and tight muscles. Applying good practice in the form of thoughtful management can go a long way to alleviating this. In addition to many of the suggestions above:

• be sensitive to situations that trigger a nervous reaction
• do not isolate him from his companions
• follow a regular routine. Horses thrive on routine. This is why they are waiting at the gate when they know it is feeding time. A regular routine reduces stress levels, which will have an impact on both physical and mental health.

Food for thought

A horse is not capable of planning ahead. He does not harbour 'naughty' or 'awkward' trains of thought. He merely reacts to a situation relying on the flight or fight instinct if frightened, uncomfortable, confused, or in pain.

We owe our horses the best possible environment in which to thrive. Whether in the field, stable, travelling or being ridden, it is up to us to ensure their comfort, welfare and safety.

This stabled horse is displaying signs of stress.

ANATOMY FOR MOVEMENT

Horses, like people, come in all shapes and sizes and none has perfect conformation. Some have the build and physiology to become gymnastic jumpers, some to race and others to become dressage horses. To succeed in any discipline, the horse must be the correct type.

This is a brief overview of some of the most important conformational points that you should consider in relation to correct movement.

What is conformation?

Conformation is the physical structure of the horse's body. It refers to bone structure, musculature and body proportions, which allow the horse to function at his optimum level. Conformation affects balance, performance and athletic potential.

Inappropriate conformation nearly always causes problems, may predispose a horse to injury, and make him uncomfortable to ride. It may also prevent a horse from fulfilling his potential.

The horse should appear to be in proportion and well balanced in all aspects of his conformation.

Some anatomical points related to movement

Poor conformation of any part of the body will affect how a horse carries himself, and how well he copes with his rider and the activities he has to perform.

Neck – the neck is important in determining the athletic ability of a horse.

- Long neck muscles help draw the foreleg forwards therefore the longer the neck, the longer the stride.
- A low set neck predisposes the horse to be heavy on the forehand.
- A higher set neck makes collection easier.
- The neck should be supple to allow bend.
- A concave neck with a thickened, rounded underline results in a high-headed horse with minimal flexion at the poll, a hollow back and limited athleticism.
- A horse that appears heavy through the neck and shoulder and light behind is likely to move on the forehand.

A high set neck.

Withers – the withers should be muscular, well-defined, extend well into the back to provide a strong fulcrum for the nuchal and supraspinous ligaments, which are involved in raising and lowering the head, neck and back.

Back – the back carries the weight of rider. It should be, strong, straight and muscular; and be supported by firm, well toned abdominal muscles.

Long back – when the distance from the withers to the tuber sacrale of the pelvis is greater than one third of the overall length of the horse, this:
• makes it more difficult for the horse to collect, shift his balance, engage the hindquarters and produce maximum thrust
• requires stronger abdominal muscles to enable elevation of the back and loins. This particularly affects upper level dressage, polo and jumping horses as it makes rapid engagement of the hindquarters difficult
• facilitates a longer galloping stride
• reduces flexion and can reduce bascule
• makes the horse a more comfortable ride.

A long backed horse.

Short back – when the distance from the withers to the tuber sacrale is less than one third of the overall length of the horse, this:
• enables the horse to change direction with ease
• tends to be stronger for carrying the weight of the rider
• may be the result of fewer thoracic vertebrae which will reduce the already limited the range of movement within the back.

Forelimbs – the front limbs determine stride length and smoothness of gaits. The two most crucial aspects are:
• the slopes and angles of bones that absorb concussion. A shoulder blade lying at 45 degrees decreases the angle between the scapula and humerus and has better shock-absorption capabilities than an upright one. It allows stride length to be maximized and provides a more comfortable ride because the rider is not over the front legs
• the straightness and trueness of the forelimbs.

This ensures wear and tear is equally distributed.

A more angled scapula slides back towards the horizontal as the horse lifts its front legs, increasing his scope over fences. A long humerus increases movement at the elbow allowing greater 'tuck' over fences and increased stride length when moving at speed.

- The longer the shoulder, the greater the area for muscle attachment to the vertebral column.
- The depth of the thoracic sling contributes to the elasticity of the forehand and the degree of absorption of concussion.
- A short humerus produces a short, choppy uncomfortable stride with increased concussion. More steps are needed to cover the ground, increasing the chance of forelimb lameness. The horse is also less adept at performing lateral movements.

A horse built with croup higher than the withers will have difficulty in collection and is predisposed to be heavy on the forehand.

A horse with long legs and sloping shoulder will move with long, flowing strides.

- A long radius with short cannon bone produces a longer stride and puts less stress on the tendons and structure of the lower leg.
- Pasterns should be of medium length, strong and sloping. Upright pasterns absorb less concussion while long sloping pasterns put undue strain on the fetlock.
- Forelegs should be straight and perpendicular when viewed from all directions. A vertical line dropped from the point of shoulder, should fall down the centre of the leg and hoof to the ground.
- Knees should be straight from both front and side views.
- The hoof should be in proportion to size of the horse with the hoof angle the same as that of the pastern. The left and right hooves should be mirror images of one another.

Hind limbs – the conformation of the hindquarters has a profound influence on athletic ability because of their role in propulsion.

- The femur should be long and slopes forward from the hip to the stifle joint, allowing the leg to come well under to increase stride length.
- The large hindquarter muscles should be well developed in order to provide maximum power, endurance and athletic ability.

- A long tibia and gaskin, together with short cannon bones and low-set hocks, allows the hocks to engage efficiently to provide the maximum stride length.
- A long gaskin ensures maximum stride length and provides maximum area for muscle attachment, a short gaskin results in decreased stride length.
- Legs should be straight and symmetrical from the hock downwards with the cannon bones parallel to optimize straight movement.
- A horse with a flexed hock will find engagement easier than a horse with a straight hock. Too straight or too flexed a hock increases the strain on the joint.
- The hock should be higher than the knee
- The hind pastern should be slightly longer than the front pastern and will be more upright.
- The angle of the hoof and pastern should be equal. Left and right hooves should be a matching pair.

SUMMARY
- Whatever his path in life, the nearer the horse is to the ideal conformation, the more likelihood there is of him moving correctly, remaining sound and fulfilling his designated role.

PAINTING HORSES

The paint that is used on the horses is harmless. It is a special brand of paint produced for young children. They would have no harmful effects were they to experiment with tasting!

All of the painting is done by the author.

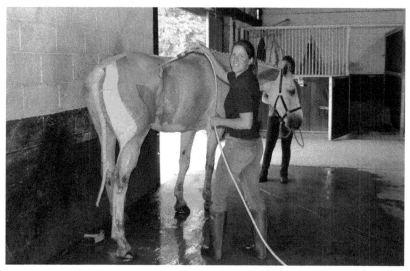

Most of the paint rubs off with a rubber curry comb and the remainder washes off easily with a gentle shampoo and warm water.

UNDERSTANDING TERMINOLOGY

Movement is often described in the following terms:

aduction – when the leg is brought out from the body

adduction – when the leg is brought across the body

asymmetrical gait – a gait in which the limb movements on one side are not exactly repeated on each side, for example, canter and gallop

cadence – rhythm combined with impulsion

impulsion – this is energy

overtracking – when the hind foot is placed in front of the imprint of the forefoot. This is a desirable quality as it denotes a supple musculature and good range of movement. With extended gaits, it is essential

rhythm – the regularity of the steps or strides in each gait. Strides should be of equal distance and duration

stride length – the distance from the placement of one hoof to where it next falls. In canter this is between 3–3.5 metres (10–12 feet)

symmetrical gait – gait in which limb movements on one side are repeated on the opposite side half a stride later, for example, the trot and pace

tempo – the speed or rhythm of the gait

tracking up – when the hind hoof steps into the imprint of the fore.

Stride phases

Stance phase – when at least one foot is in contact with the ground. This can be further subdivided into:

- initial ground contact – heel or flat foot in slow gaits, heel first in fast gaits, and toe first in some dressage moves, such as piaffe
- impact phase – rapid deceleration immediately following initial ground contact. The muscles do not have time to completely protect the joints at this point, so concussion is at its maximum
- loading phase – the body passes over the foot. The tendons and suspensory ligaments are stretched and the fetlock sinks towards the ground
- breakover – the point at which the heels leave the ground. On hard ground the foot stays flat until the heel leaves the ground. On soft ground the foot rotates as the toe digs in to the ground. This puts less pressure on the bones of the foot
- toe off – the point at which the toe leaves the ground allowing the tendons to recoil.

Swing phase – when the hoof is lifted and brought forward in a pendulum action. The forelimb pivots around the upper part of the scapula while the hind limb pivots around the hip joint in walk and trot and the lumbo-sacral joint in canter and gallop.

Suspension phase – when no hooves are in contact with the ground, for example, mid-stride in the faster paces.

Directional terms

Caudal	Towards the tail
Cranial	Towards the skull
Distal	Away from the point of attachment
Dorsal	Towards the top
Lateral	Towards the side of the body
Medial	Towards the midline of the body
Proximal	Towards the point of attachment
Ventral	Towards the underside

INDEX

Printed in the USA
CPSIA information can be obtained
at www.ICGtesting.com
JSHW072027140824
68134JS00043B/3818